Partners in Need

The Strategic Relationship
of Russia and Iran

Brenda Shaffer

Policy Paper no. 57

THE WASHINGTON INSTITUTE FOR NEAR EAST POLICY

© 2001 by the Washington Institute for Near East Policy

Published in 2001 in the United States of America by the Washington Institute for Near East Policy, 1828 L Street NW, Suite 1050, Washington, DC 20036.

Library of Congress Cataloging-in-Publication Data

Shaffer, Brenda.
Partners in need: The strategic relationship of Russia and Iran/ Brenda Shaffer
            p. cm. — (Policy papers ; no. 57)
     Includes bibliographical references
     ISBN 0-944029-48-5(pbk.)
     ISBN 0-944029-48-5
  1. Russia (Federation)–Relations–Iran. 2.Iran–Relations–Russia (Federation) 3. United States–Foreign relations–1993-. 4.Middle East–Relations–Foreign countries.
I. Title. II. Series: Policy papers (Washington Institute for Near East Policy); 58.
 DK68.7.S53 2001
 327.47055–dc21

                   2001001364
                   CIP

Cover photo: Russian president Vladimir Putin (L) and his Iranian counterpart Mohammad Khatami shake hands during their meeting in the Kremlin, March12, 2001.

© Archive Photo. Cover design by Alicia Gansz.

The Author

Brenda Shaffer is research director at Harvard University's Caspian Studies Program and was a visiting fellow at The Washington Institute in 2000. Dr. Shaffer is a specialist in Russian–Iranian relations, the Caucasus, Central Asia, and ethnic politics in Iran. She is the author of a forthcoming book on Azerbaijani identity (MIT Press, September 2001) and is currently researching a study on the link between culture and foreign policy, drawing on cases from the Caspian region.

● ● ●

Table of Contents

Acknowledgments

I wish to thank The Washington Institute and its executive director, Robert Satloff, for giving me the opportunity to address this topic. I am indebted to Patrick Clawson for his excellent professional guidance. Alicia Gansz and John Grennan also helped prepare this Policy Paper for publication.

Much of the research for this project was conducted while I was in residence at the Belfer Center for Science and International Affairs at Harvard University's Kennedy School of Government. I greatly appreciate the academic home and research guidance provided to me there by Graham Allison and Steven Miller, and the support from the Caspian Studies Program at Harvard University. I am especially grateful to Matt Bunn from the Belfer Center, who invested hours of his time guiding me through proliferation issues and made extensive comments on this paper. I also thank Ambassador Robert Galluci, Robert Freedman, and Michael Eisenstadt for their important comments.

Brenda Shaffer
May 2001

Preface

Why does secular Russia, enmeshed in a bloody war against Chechen Islamist–inspired rebels, agree to sell massive amounts of arms to the Islamist regime in Iran and help that regime to develop a nuclear industry? U.S. officials have often been perplexed at the difficulties they face in trying to prevent Russian proliferation of destabilizing military technologies to Iran.

In this incisive Policy Paper, Caspian Basin specialist Brenda Shaffer presents a comprehensive overview of how Russia and Iran view each other, providing a detailed explanation of why Russia does not share all U.S. concerns about Iranian actions. This issue raises significant policy questions for the U.S. government and has been discussed repeatedly at the highest levels—not least during the work of the Gore–Chernomyrdin Commission. Several U.S. laws have also offered both carrots and sticks to secure Russian cooperation—tying cooperation to cash for Russia's space program and conversion of its nuclear arsenal, while sanctioning Russian entities that engage in proliferation.

Dr. Shaffer, research director at Harvard University's Caspian Studies Program and a visiting fellow at The Washington Institute in 2000, uses her rich command of the Russian literature on Iran to show why the United States has had only limited success with these efforts. She argues that because Russia views its relations and cooperation with Iran as vital to national security, it will not jeopardize those relations for the sake of short-term material incentives or out of fear of U.S. condemnation. This analysis complements the Institute's recent Policy Paper by Dr. Eugene Rumer, *Dangerous Drift: Russia's Middle East Policy* (2000), which argues that the corporate greed, lack of bureaucratic restraint, and relaxed views on proliferation apparent in Russia today mean that Moscow is unlikely to become a reliable partner in the fight against proliferation.

Formulating an effective policy to prevent Iran from acquiring dangerous military technologies from Russian sources requires an understanding of how one partner views the other. To advance that goal, The Washington Institute is proud to present this important and timely research.

Michael Stein
Chairman

Fred S. Lafer
President

Executive Summary

Russia and Iran are neighboring states. As such, the status of their bilateral relationship is a perpetually important facet of their respective foreign policies. In the post-Soviet period, Tehran and Moscow began to view and term their cooperation as "strategic"—each side viewing the other as integral to its own national security, internal stability, and territorial integrity.

Presently, Russia and Iran also view their cooperative relationship as an important tool toward three ends: preventing U.S. hegemony in world affairs; maintaining what Tehran and Moscow refer to as a "multipolar" world; and undermining U.S. efforts to sideline or boycott either of them. Indeed, since the fall of the Soviet Union, Moscow has viewed its relations with Iran as a manifestation of its own independence from the West. Russia does not share U.S. concerns regarding Iran in adjacent regional zones, but rather views Tehran as a strategic partner, especially in Central Asia and the Caucasus. Moreover, Moscow views the preservation of ties and cooperation with Iran—a state that has problematic relations with the West—as a means of ensuring that Russian interests in the Middle East and Caspian regions will be taken into consideration.

Russia does not believe that it shares common interests with the United States in the sphere of combating the threat posed by some Islamist groups. From the Russian viewpoint, Islamist-based security threats emanate principally from nonstate-sponsored groups in Western-oriented states like Saudi Arabia, Pakistan, and Turkey.

Additionally, Moscow views cooperation with Tehran as essential for preventing a Muslim backlash in response to Russian actions in Chechnya: the official Iranian view of the conflict as an internal Russian affair undermines Muslim efforts to band together against Moscow. Moscow policymakers view other regional powers such as Turkey as more threatening to Russian interests than Iran. Nevertheless, Moscow's policies demonstrate that it views Tehran as potentially threatening to important Russian interests. For instance, Russia's Federal Security Service (FSB) has targeted Iranian efforts to acquire from Russia technologies and materials that could advance its nuclear weapons programs.

For its part, Iran's geopolitical interests with Russia have taken precedence over its Islamic agenda. As far as Tehran is concerned, Russia's actions against Muslims in Chechnya and in other arenas are secondary in the context of Iran's overall strategic agenda. Although Tehran has decided to cooperate with Moscow on certain issues, it does not seem to entirely trust its northern neighbor. Moreover, many Iranians outside the policy community perceive Russia as potentially threatening.

In the Caspian region, although Russia and Iran cooperated throughout most of the 1990s (united by their mutual goal of preventing an expanded U.S. presence in the region), they are nevertheless potential competitors as important oil producers and prospective alternative transit routes for the region's oil and gas reserves.

In the past decade, Iran has made significant progress in its programs for acquiring weapons of mass destruction (WMD), especially vis-à-vis missile capability. Russian companies and government ministries have played an important role in advancing these capabilities—especially in Iran's ballistic missile program. U.S. pressure has failed to significantly alter the pace or level of Russian–Iranian cooperation in this regard; in fact, U.S. exhortation has turned the matter of cooperation into a symbolic issue, and Russian concessions have consequently become more costly and difficult to extract. Moscow believes that halting its cooperation with Iran in these fields would constitute a concession to Washington—a perception that underscores the failure of U.S. policy on this issue.

The overall framework of Russian commitment to the United States regarding military cooperation with Iran broke down on the eve of the U.S. presidential election in 2000 when Russia abrogated its agreement not to conclude any new conventional arms deals with Iran after 1999. The Russian announcement was followed by Marshal Igor Sergeyev's visit to Tehran in December 2000—the first visit of a Russian defense minister to Iran since 1980—and Iranian president Mohammad Khatami's landmark visit to Russia in March 2001. Iranian acquisition capabilities have been further energized by rising oil prices and by Russian assertion of an independent foreign policy. These new Iranian capabilities will place Russian–Iranian strategic cooperation on the Bush administration's agenda of major foreign policy challenges.

Grasping the depth and significance of Russian–Iranian relations is pivotal to determining what kind of influence can best elicit Moscow's cooperation in preventing the transfer of materials and technologies that advance Iranian programs for WMD development. Russia's cooperation with Iran in this field does not stem solely, or even primarily, from financial reasons. Because Russia views its relations and cooperation with Iran as important to national security, it will not jeopardize those relations for the sake of short-term material incentives or fear of U.S. condemnation. Furthermore, any U.S. attempt to link Russia's cooperation in this sphere with programs that are more important to the United States than to Russia—such as the processing and storage of Russia's fissile materials—is unlikely to be effective. In this regard, Washington's threat to cancel such programs in retaliation for Moscow's cooperation with Tehran is not credible, and the United States thereby risks a double setback: it may have to forfeit programs that it values, while Russian cooperation with Iran continues unabated. Even though material incentives and penalties are not effective in preventing Moscow's overall strategic cooperation with Tehran, they have nevertheless been useful in influencing the behavior of specific Russian institutes and factories.

If cooperation develops between the United States and Iran, then a dramatic shift in the nature of relations between Russia and Iran could occur. Despite its own declarations to the contrary, Russia would stand to lose the most if there is a significant rapprochement between Tehran and Washington. Moscow will therefore work to prevent and undermine this possibility.

Chapter 1

Introduction

Throughout the past decade, Russian–Iranian cooperation in the nuclear sphere has puzzled the Washington policy community and academic researchers. Moscow often discovers Iranian attempts to obtain equipment, technology, and materials related to weapons of mass destruction (WMD) illicitly, yet it does little to stop these efforts. In fact, Moscow officially cooperates with Iran on nominally civilian nuclear projects that actually provide Iran with opportunities to advance its military programs. Russia and Iran are neighboring states, and Tehran's acquisition of nuclear weapons would significantly change the strategic balance in the region they share. Moreover, Moscow is oppressing Muslims in Chechnya, and both Russia and Iran want influence among the Muslim peoples of Central Asia and the Caucasus. Wouldn't these factors seem to put these two states on a collision course and cause Moscow to believe that Iran's acquisition of WMD threatens its own security?

To understand the drive behind Russian–Iranian cooperation and the measures that can be used to address this challenge, we must recognize that Iran and Russia share a number of top-level strategic priorities. Tehran and Moscow view their mutual relations as an integral component of their respective national security policies. These relations carry important implications for each country's domestic security and stability as well.

There are a number of points that are crucial to understanding relations between Russia and Iran. First, Iran has on some issues been extremely pragmatic. When its geopolitical interests in relations with Russia collide with its Islamic agenda, state interests almost always take precedence. As far as Tehran is concerned, Russia's actions against Muslims in Chechnya and beyond are secondary to pursuing Iran's strategic agenda. More to the point, Russia has resources and technology that Iran wants. Also, Iranian cooperation with Russia could help offset U.S. hegemony in the international arena, and together Iran and Russia could prevent the expansion of the U.S. presence and influence in the region they both border. In addition, Moscow's vulnerability in Chechnya is pivotal to understanding its cooperation with Iran on military and nuclear issues. The Iranian government and media were quite mild in their criticism of Russia during the Chechen wars, considering the Muslim background of the Chechen rebels. Iran's criticisms were confined to the rhetorical level, and the solid cooperation between Moscow and Tehran was never disturbed by disagreements over Chechnya.

In fact, because Iran has helped to prevent a Muslim backlash against Russia's actions in Chechnya, Moscow has reciprocated with public affirmations of its commitment to cooperate with Iran in the nuclear and security spheres. As long as Russia is involved in a conflict with Chechnya, it will do little to upset its relationship with Tehran. Thus, it is futile for the United States to base its nonproliferation efforts vis-à-vis Iran on Russia's agreement to work actively to prevent Iran's acquisition of nuclear technologies and materials. The United States may be able to convince Russia to refrain from providing the equipment and technologies most directly applicable to nuclear weapons, but Russia will not cut off its broader military and nuclear cooperation with Iran unless the United States offers concessions that affect top Russian strategic interests.

Russian foreign minister Igor Ivanov announced in November 2000 that Moscow's previous commitments to the United States to suspend arms sales to Iran were null and void—a clear signal that Moscow is no longer interested in serving as a contractor for the United States on arms issues and that the United States must develop a new policy. This Russian announcement was followed by Marshal Igor

Sergeyev's trip to Tehran in December 2000, the first visit of a Russian defense minister to Iran since 1980.

This work examines Russian–Iranian relations and cooperation in the post-Soviet period. Chapter 2 provides background for the general framework of Russian–Iranian relations: their history, their views of one another, and the policymakers and institutions that influence their policies toward one another. Chapter 3 deals with their contemporary cooperation and relations in the political, security, and economic arenas. Chapter 4 examines arms deals and strategic weapons cooperation between Russia and Iran. Chapter 5 provides policy prescriptions based on an assessment of these relations.

Chapter 2
Framework of Relations

O ne of the most important elements in the relations between Iran and Russia is geography: the two are neighboring states, and, for the predominant part of their history,
have shared a common border. Russia and Iran have inter-
acted for a long time, and have often been obliged to craft
policies toward one another. Because they are bordering
states, the internal developments, military strategies, and
posture of each has affected the bilateral relationship between
them, even if these factors were not directly connected with
or intended to influence the bilateral track. Russia's relations
with Iran have always differed greatly from the West's. From
Russia's perspective, Iran is not a country far abroad or in the
Third World, but rather one looming on its own border.

Iran and Russia's history of interaction as adjacent states
has created positive and negative legacies for both countries.
Their respective regional aspirations have frequently brought
them into confrontation. They have vied for territory in the
border zone between them, and the boundary between the
two countries has changed a number of times. Because Russia has usually held the upper hand in territorial
confrontations, Moscow and Tehran have inherited different
residual attitudes toward one another: Russia tends to feel
rather confident, Iran rather defensive. In addition, throughout the 1800s and the first half of the 1900s, Moscow was often
directly involved in Iranian domestic affairs, further reinforcing its threatening image.

In the early nineteenth century, through a series of confrontations, Iran lost the Caucasus to tsarist Russia, a
development formalized in the 1813 Treaty of Gulistan and
the 1828 Treaty of Turkmenchay. Iran became a pawn in the

5

British–Russian competition in the region and was divided by their respective spheres of influence. Yet despite the territorial clashes between Iran and Russia, they are neighbors first and foremost. As such, trade naturally developed between them, and trade has remained a constant feature in their interaction.

Imperial Russia (and subsequently the Soviet Union) intervened in Iranian affairs on a number of occasions, and these events have had a lingering affect on contemporary Iranian feelings toward Russia. Among those incursions, Soviet troops landed on the Iranian shore of the Caspian Sea in 1920. At that time, a number of local autonomy movements were contending with the Iranian central authorities of the Qajar Dynasty in the north of Iran. Moscow withdrew its troops within a year, having negotiated a favorable Treaty of Friendship with the nascent Pahlavi regime. Soviet troops returned to Iran in 1941, as part of the Allied occupation during World War II. British forces occupied southern Iran during this period, while Soviet troops were present in the north, and the two sides compelled the abdication of Shah Reza Pahlavi. Britain withdrew its troops from Iran at the end of World War II, and the Soviet troops remained in the north for an additional year, withdrawing in May 1946.

During 1945 and 1946, two provisional governments that represented ethnic-based autonomy movements were established in the north of Iran, in Azerbaijan and Kurdistan. Most Western accounts and Iranian historiography of these revolts and short-lived provincial governments present them as Soviet puppet states—the result of the Soviet military presence in Iran, rather than as locally based phenomena.[1] Although it is important to understand how Iranians viewed these autonomy movements in recognizing their effect on the Iranian view of the Soviet Union, evidently these revolts had a much larger grassroots support and motivation than was surmised. Soviet support was clearly essential in providing opportunity and tools for these two governments, but many of the goals and demands of the provincial government in Iranian

Azerbaijan were primarily local. Initially, popular support for the provincial government was quite extensive,[2] and most of the local population supported the measures taken in the spheres of economy, infrastructure, and status of the Azerbaijani language.

In contrast with most outside references to the provincial government in Azerbaijan, its leaders never referred to it as the Azerbaijan Democratic Republic (ADR)—that is, as a separate country. They declared in their first statement, for example, that the Azerbaijanis were a distinct nation (*millet*), but that they were not aiming for the secession of Azerbaijan from Iran. They voiced three major demands: the use of the Azerbaijani language in local schools and government offices, the retention of tax revenues for the development of the region, and the establishment of the provincial assemblies promised in the constitutional laws.[3]

A number of treaties signed between the Soviet Union and Iran became important milestones in their relationship. The 1921 Treaty of Friendship is still a subject of contention between Iran and Russia. It contains a number of clauses that were later cited as legal justification for Soviet interventions in Iran—including the 1941 Soviet occupation of northern Iran, which was part of the Allied takeover of the country.[4] In 1940, the Soviet Union and Iran signed an additional major treaty. Despite the renunciation of both treaties by the shah's regime and their subsequent abrogation by the Islamic Republic, both Tehran and Moscow have often invoked aspects of these treaties when it served their own interests. For example, both sides have used the 1921 and 1940 treaties to justify their positions on the status of the Caspian Sea.[5]

In the Soviet period, Moscow's policy toward Iran reflected its view of that country as a neighbor rather than as part of the Third World or the Middle East. Because of its pivotal location, Iran was contested in the U.S.–Soviet Cold War rivalry. Iran's arms buildup in the 1970s and its significant ties with the United States were of serious concern to the Soviets, who felt themselves to be on the defensive. Moreover, because of the importance of the Persian Gulf to the United States,

Moscow placed a high priority on this region and sought to thwart further U.S. successes there.

As part of its policy for gaining wider influence in Iran, Moscow often supported and fostered ties with regional and ethnic autonomy movements there. Iran is a multi-ethnic state, and approximately 50 percent of its citizens are non-Persian. The largest minority group is the Azerbaijanis, who make up close to a third of the country's population. Other major groups include the Kurds, Arabs, Baluchs, and Turkmen. Many of these groups are concentrated in Iran's frontier areas, and most have ties to co-ethnics in the adjoining states of Azerbaijan, Turkmenistan, Pakistan, and Turkey. Consequently, Iran's ethnic groups are especially subject to the influence of events taking place in these bordering states, and the ethnic question is not merely a domestic matter.

During the Soviet period, Moscow's policy toward these movements in Iran—especially that of the Azerbaijanis—was highly influenced by the presence of the same groups in the Soviet Union. Many Soviet Azerbaijanis supported the autonomy of their co-ethnics in Iran and desired increased ties with them. Fear of Moscow, however, actually inhibited political activity among many of the ethnic groups in Iran. Many activists voiced a concern that secessionist movements would only increase their vulnerability to Soviet dictates, observing that they were not interested in "trading one dictator for another." Thus, the perception of a looming Soviet threat often deterred ethnic-based political activity in Iran.

Another potential source of Soviet influence in Iran was the Iranian Communist movement, especially the Tudeh Party. In the post–World War II period, the Tudeh was both an asset and a liability for the USSR. On the one hand, it gave the Soviet Union access to certain information and contacts, as well as limited political leverage. On the other hand, Moscow's connections to the movement were somewhat of an obstacle, as they reinforced the image of the Soviet Union as an intruder in domestic Iranian affairs. Furthermore, the USSR's failure to assist the Tudeh led to the loss of Soviet prestige.

These connections were problematic for the Tudeh as well. Its closeness with the USSR tainted it with the image of being a foreign tool that was not loyal to Iranian interests. Moreover, at many junctures Moscow sacrificed its ties to the Tudeh, along with the safety of its leaders, in order to improve its state-to-state relations with Iran. Rarely did the Soviet media mention the shah's repression of Communists in Iran, and Moscow gave little assistance in the 1960s and 1970s to Tudeh activists exiled in East Germany.[6] Moscow was also cautious in its attitude toward the Iranian anti-Western movement led by Muhammad Mossadeq (1951–1953). Even though Mossadeq allowed the Tudeh to operate while he served as prime minister of Iran, and advocated socialist-oriented policies such as the nationalization of Iran's oil industry, the Soviets neither embraced Mossadeq nor his ideology.

A further instrument of Soviet influence in Iran was the "National Voice of Iran" radio service, founded in 1959 and broadcast from Baku in Soviet Azerbaijan in both Farsi and Azerbaijani. Many Iranian Azerbaijanis also listened to Radio Baku, which broadcast mainly in the Azerbaijani language.

Despite Iran's ties to the United States during the Pahlavi regime, the Soviet Union's ties to Iraq, and the presence of radical groups in the Persian Gulf, the 1,250-mile Soviet–Iranian border was stable throughout most of the post–World War II period—until the eve of the collapse of the Soviet Union. Trade was also very strong between the Soviet Union and Iran during this period. By fostering cooperation with the Soviets, Tehran improved its bargaining position with Washington and increased pressure on the United States to meet its demands for arms. In the 1960s and 1970s, trade between the USSR and Iran expanded dramatically, as Iran became the largest market for Soviet nonmilitary goods in the Middle East and the Soviets' third-largest trading partner in the Third World (after Egypt and India).[7]

At the height of these two countries' cooperation, 3,000 Soviet technical advisors were working in Iran, and in 1967, Iran began purchasing a limited supply of arms from the Soviet Union. The Soviets also provided credit for the Isfahan Steel Works—after the United States refused to fund this project—and it became a major Soviet showpiece. As part of a major agreement in 1970, Iran built a natural gas pipeline to the Soviet Union. By using this Iranian gas for Soviet domestic consumption, the USSR was able to increase its own gas exports to the West. A second pipeline—under negotiation prior to the fall of the Pahlavi regime— was scrapped after the Islamic Revolution.

The Islamic Revolution caught Moscow, like its Western counterparts, by surprise. Because of Ayatollah Ruhollah Khomeini's fervent anti-American policies and rhetoric, Moscow welcomed the revolution and the new regime. Attempting to create a sense of ideological affinity between the regimes, Moscow stressed the anti-imperialist aspects of the ayatollah's agenda. This stance was reflected in the official Soviet media, and many articles in the Soviet press attributed a "progressive character" to Islam. Leonid Brezhnev stated in his February 1981 address to the Twentieth-Sixth Congress of the Communist Party of the Soviet Union (CPSU) that the "liberation struggle can unfold under the banner of Islam."[8]

The Soviet press also supported the Iranian takeover of the U.S. embassy in Tehran. During the early Khomeini period, the USSR courted Tehran and encouraged the Tudeh to support the new regime. In 1980 and 1981, the Soviet Union doubled its trade with Iran. Khomeini's "neither East nor West" policy, while nominally anti-Soviet, was actually an improvement for Moscow over the pro-American stance of the shah's regime. Despite Soviet overtures, however, Khomeini did little to reciprocate and made few concessions in his anti-Soviet rhetoric. Early points of contention between the Islamic Republic and the Soviet Union centered on the price of gas Iran supplied to the USSR, as well as the Soviet invasion of Afghanistan. Not only did Iran object to the latter on ideological grounds, but the Soviet occupation also produced a flood of refugees into Iran, and fostered fears about further Soviet designs on the area.

The advent of the Iran–Iraq War pitted Iran, which Moscow was attempting to court, against Iraq, which was already a Soviet partner, thus creating a difficult situation for the USSR. The Soviet position on the war during the period from 1980 to 1982 tilted in favor of Iran. They subsequently adopted a more balanced position, perhaps in response to the Iranian military successes of July 1982 that threatened the Iraqi regime of Saddam Husayn. Despite Moscow's efforts to assuage both sides, its relationship with Tehran plummeted in the early months of 1983 when Khomeini's regime arrested, tried, and executed Tudeh Party activists and then expelled Soviet diplomats.

Under Mikhail Gorbachev, the Soviet Union made a number of gestures to improve its relations with Iran. Despite Moscow's official praise of Iran, Khomeini sent a letter to Gorbachev in early 1989 instructing him to adopt Islam as a cure for the Soviet Union's problems. The letter also stressed the Soviet Union and Iran's shared concerns about the onslaught of Western culture. Ultimately, three factors facilitated a dramatic improvement in the relations between Iran and the Soviet Union: Moscow's contribution to a ceasefire agreement between Iran and Iraq and the realization of that ceasefire; the Soviet withdrawal from Afghanistan; and the general liberalization in Iran following Khomeini's death in 1989.

Directly after the Soviet withdrawal from Afghanistan, Soviet foreign minister Eduard Shevardnadze visited Iran in February 1989. This event was followed in June by the landmark visit of the Speaker of the *Majlis* (parliament), Akbar Hashemi Rafsanjani, to Moscow. On that occasion, Iran and Russia signed agreements dealing with arms supplies and, for the first time, for cooperation in the field of nuclear energy.[9]

According to the Iranian press, military officers in the Soviet delegation committed their government to supplying weapons to Iran sufficient to meet that country's defense needs[10] and gave an undefined commitment to help Iran "strengthen its defense capability." The latter appeared in the

Declaration on the Principles of Relations between the USSR and Iran, signed during the visit.[11] Rafsanjani traveled from Moscow to Baku, Azerbaijan, where he made it clear that Iran intended to relate to the Soviet Muslim republics through Moscow.

Prior to the dissolution of the Soviet Union, Iran was somewhat critical of Soviet policies toward Muslims in the USSR and encouraged ties between the Muslim peoples of Central Asia and the Caucasus and the citizens of Iran.[12] Tehran did not regard the collapse of the Soviet Union as an advantageous development. Taken by surprise,[13] Tehran was slow to recognize the new states and clung to its support of Moscow's hegemony until acknowledgment of the demise of the USSR was inevitable. The *Tehran Times* commented in August 1991:

> The Islamic Republic [also has] very good relations with the central Soviet Government, and does not desire to witness any weakening of President Gorbachev's government . . . From a general geopolitical point of view, Iran believes that the disintegration of the Soviet Union will result in an undesirable wave of instability in the region, and for that reason Iran is against some of the extremist nationalistic movements of some of the republics of the Soviet Union.[14]

The newspaper went on to state unequivocally that "Tehran is not happy with Gorbachev's exit from the political arena," and that the country sought to forge relations with the new states "within the framework of relations with Moscow."[15] The Soviet collapse led to the emergence of a unipolar world under U.S. hegemony. States such as Iran had benefited from the superpower competition, which had increased their importance and their ability to acquire resources. Iran grasped that its once-stable northern border had become a conflict-ridden zone, and that influences from the new states could permeate the internal Iranian arena.

After the Soviet demise, Iran began to place limitations on direct ties between Iranians and the people of some of the new states, especially the people of Azerbaijan. Soon after the Soviet breakup, Iranian hardliners recognized that Azerbaijan had a pro-Western and specifically pro-Turkish orientation—thus, its independence created only limited opportunity for Iran to expand its influence.[16] Moreover, Tehran was sensitive to assertions of Azerbaijani ethnic identity and feared that Baku could exert a pull over the Azerbaijanis in Iran. This concern had a major impact on Iran's policy toward the Caucasus and Russia.

Russia's View of Iran

Although Moscow policymakers do view Iran with a degree of caution, they see other regional powers such as Turkey as potentially more threatening to Russian interests. Observers in Moscow see Iran as a state whose ideology affects only the policies of certain factions. Most Russians perceive that even in instances of confrontation, Russia succeeds in imposing its will on Iran and in defusing many of its policies. Hence, cooperation with Iran is generally viewed as the best means to bring about Tehran's acquiescence to Russia's needs.

Russia sees the regime in Iran as being highly fractionalized, and many of its public institutions as independent from the main sources of power in Tehran. Senior Russian policymakers have frequently expressed this view. For instance, former Foreign Minister Andrei Kozyrev remarked:

> There is no doubt that Rafsanjani and Foreign Minister ['Ali Akbar] Velayati are representatives of the moderate wing, and they are trying to move away from tough Islamic fundamentalism. But it must not be forgotten that there is a second stratum, a shadowy stage on which completely different forces operate.[17]

Moscow's view of this dual nature of the Iranian government allows it to tolerate policies it views as threatening—such as Muslim agitation in Russia or Central Asia, or illicit attempts to acquire technologies or components of weapons of mass destruction (WMD). It views these actions as the work of independent organizations over which the central government has no control.[18]

Despite Moscow's rhetoric of friendship with Iran and its criticism of Washington's Iran policy, Moscow's policies demonstrate that it views Tehran as potentially threatening to important Russian interests and Russian security. For example, in 1999, during the second Chechen war, Russia blocked the entry of Iranian trucks heading for Europe by way of the North Caucasus region.[19] In addition, Iran was among the Muslim countries whose goods were subject to special customs control regulations imposed in December 1999.[20] These measures were part of a Russian government resolution designated "On Measures for Preventing the Penetration of Foreign Terrorist Organization Members, the Shipment of Arms and Instruments of Sabotage onto Russian Territory through Border Checkpoints in North Caucasus Region." Moreover, it appears that the Russian Federal Security Service (FSB) targets Iranian efforts to acquire from Russia technologies and materials that could advance Tehran's nuclear weapons programs. The FSB has publicly announced its success in foiling a number of such attempts. (See chapter 3 for a discussion of Iran's attempts to acquire technology and materials for its WMD programs.)

Russian military and security officers often identify Iran as a threat to Russian security. Russian military journals frequently refer to the "threat from the south" as a focus of the post-Soviet military mission. They do not usually mention Iran explicitly, but occasionally do so. Members of the Russian military and security establishment are more likely than civilian policymakers to refer to Iran as a potential threat.[21] President Boris Yeltsin, however, in what appeared to be extemporaneous remarks, occasionally referred to Iran as a source of support for "terrorist activity" in the Caucasus.[22]

Journalists and Russian popular opinion often reflexively identified Iran as a potential culprit in the terrorist attacks in Russia in 1999 and as a backer of other Islamic, anti-Russian forces in the former Soviet Union, illustrating an inherent popular distrust of Iran. Moreover, in discussions about the threat of Islamic extremism, Iran is often mentioned as a source of risk, along with Saudi Arabia, Pakistan, and Turkey.

At times, the Russian media refer to it as a source of international terror.[23] Various journalists have described Iran in very negative terms, using the term "fanatic," for example, in an article criticizing attacks by Iranians on female Russian construction workers at the nuclear plant in Bushehr, Iran.[24]

Russian officials point out that cooperation exists between Moscow and Tehran, but that it is affected by the fundamentally different cultural norms of each society. For example, in an article that appeared in the Russian foreign policy journal *International Affairs,* the author discussed how province-to-province cooperation is hampered by what he described as "Islamic bans on some forms of recreation and entertainment."[25]

Russian policymakers are divided over the degree to which Iran engages in destabilizing activity among the Muslim populations of Russia, Central Asia, and the Caucasus. Nevertheless, even those who postulate that Iran is active in this sphere claim that the best way to thwart such activity is by cooperating with Iran. Russian research and policy communities overwhelmingly view a greater Muslim threat from states with a Western orientation, such as Pakistan, Saudi Arabia, and Turkey. Moscow believes that because its trade and security ties with Tehran allow it to moderate Iranian behavior, it does not need to be alarmed by Iranian ties to Muslim groups in the region. In fact, there have been times when Russia even approved of Iran's ties to rebel groups (such as in Tajikistan), because they created an additional lever for influence and prevented rebel collaboration with forces over which Moscow could not control.

Russian policymakers, journalists, and academics tend to distinguish between "Islamic fundamentalism" and "Islamic extremism."[26] Those who have discussed this division, including former Prime Minister Yevgenii Primakov, claim that fundamentalist regimes like Iran, which are basically religious societies, should be differentiated from extremist ones like Afghanistan, which actively engage in destabilizing activities in other states. It is not clear, however, whether this distinction accurately reflects Russian perceptions or merely serves Russian rhetorical purposes.

Iran's View of Russia

Iranian policymakers view Russia as sharing many common interests with Iran. They are cautious, however, in their judgment of some of Russia's intentions. Although Tehran has made a strategic decision in favor of cooperation with Moscow, it does not seem to trust its northern neighbor. On the grassroots level and among intellectuals outside the policy community, many Iranians perceive Russia as potentially threatening and harboring expansionist desires toward their country. Russia's support for the various ethnic-based autonomy movements that emerged in Iran during the twentieth century, they point out, demonstrates its irredentist tendencies toward its neighbor.

These analysts perceive Russia's foreign policy elite as fragmented—which mirrors Russian policymakers' view of Iran's foreign policy establishment. It is guided, they believe, by bureaucratic politics, with diverse institutions attempting to implement diverse policies. For instance, with regard to Tajikistan, Iranian officials have commented on the differing policies of the Russian Foreign Ministry and the Russian Ministry of Defense.[27]

Iranians view Russian technology and goods as inferior to U.S. products, especially military hardware and technology.[28] But Iranian officials give precedence to the fact that Russia and Iran are both economic "have-nots." Moreover, some postulate that Iran and Russia are compatible trading partners because of the two countries' common economic level, and so it is preferable for Iran to buy Russian goods and technology that may not be top of the line but are significantly less expensive.[29]

Iran perceives Russia as the dominant power in Central Asia and the Caucasus, and it believes that Russia's presence and influence are essential to maintaining regional stability and curbing an expanded Western presence in this border area. Yet despite this sense of partnership and common interests, Tehran does not want a return of Russian troops to the border zones between Azerbaijan and Iran or Turkmenistan and Iran. Some Iranian newspapers have even described Russia's intentions in Central Asia as "expansionist."[30]

Iranian policymakers view both Russia and Iran as states struggling against a Western cultural onslaught, and many have expressed respect for Russian culture, especially in comparison to that of the United States. According to Abbas Maleki, who participated in the Iranian–Russian roundtables:

> With regard to the development of international cultural cooperation, we have repeatedly stressed the essence of our late Leader's letter to Mikhail Gorbachev, reiterating the inadmissibility of the spread of Western culture and behavior. The Russian and Iranian nations enjoy an incomparable cultural edge, a factor that can set cultural precedents the world over. . . . Russia and Iran enjoy enough cultural wealth and credibility to launch a whole new campaign for the initiation of novel cultural policies.[31]

Self-Perceptions

Relations between Russia and Iran are highly influenced by the way each of these states sees itself. Russia considers itself to be a great power that is passing through a period of weakness, but one that will command a central political role in the future. It is proud of its culture and does not feel inferior to the United States. Iran views itself as a regional power with an important culture, especially in relation to other states and societies in the contiguous Muslim world.

In their contacts, Tehran and Moscow treat each other as powerful and important countries whose interests should be respected. This mutual perception, which more closely approximates their self-images than the West's images of them, contributes to their successful relations. Kamal Kharrazi recognized this mutual respect in an article he wrote prior to his appointment as foreign minister of Iran:

> The common portrayal of Russia as a destitute and second-class state is misleading and inconsistent with a global strategic vision. Despite economic hardship and internal po-

litical upheaval, Russia has been successful in communicating to the world both in words and in deeds that it rejects being regarded as second class and that it will pursue its national interests beyond its borders.[32]

Policymakers and Institutions

Bureaucratic politics have had a significant impact on Iran and Russia's policies toward each other, especially in the chief region of their interaction—Central Asia and the Caucasus. Various institutions in each state influence policy toward the other, often creating inconsistency and incoherence. Tehran's policy toward Russia and the adjoining regions illustrates the diversity of opinion and extensive pluralism of the foreign policymaking process in Iran.[33] For example, the Iranian newspaper *Jomhuri-ye Islami*, which represents the view of Islamic hardliners, has frequently published articles criticizing the Iranian Ministry of Foreign Affairs for taking an appeasement position toward Russia's actions in the Chechnya and Karabagh conflicts and for not sufficiently supporting the pro-Islamic forces in Tajikistan.[34] *Kayhan International* has also been critical of Russia's policies and Iran's acceptance of them.

Russia's responses to Iranian actions in Tajikistan in the early 1990s revealed the pluralism within the Moscow policy elite. Defense Ministry representatives frequently criticized Iran, which was providing aid to the Tajik insurgents fighting Russian soldiers. At the same time, the Russian Foreign Ministry praised the Islamic Republic, and even its activities in Tajikistan, in the hopes of fostering Iranian cooperation in Central Asia. Russia's position regarding the Caspian Sea and its cooperation with Iran on this issue was influenced by various institutions with opposing interests. For example, the Foreign Ministry emphasized the importance of a consistent legal position, while the oil company Lukoil and the Ministry of Fuel and Energy often ignored the official position (frequently to the chagrin of Tehran) when opportunities arose to participate in Caspian energy projects.

Moscow's cooperation with Iran is often the topic of domestic political debates in Russia. Commentators Yuri Melnikov and Vladimir Frolov observed:

> [Regarding] the influence of both an internal political consensus and the logic of the electoral struggle in Russia: today no serious political force can advocate unilateral and unjustified concessions to the [United States] that would hurt Russian manufacturers. In addition, Russia has other important interests in developing relations with neighboring Iran.[35]

Ties with Iran, including extensive cooperation in the civil nuclear field, are popular among a wide array of political factions in Russia. The Communists and many right-wing groups consider a policy of strong cooperation to be pivotal for Russia to maintain its independence from U.S. dictates. When Boris Yeltsin came under domestic pressure and criticism for his subservience to U.S. policies, he often responded by pointing to Russia's relations with Iran in response, thus endowing those relations with extra significance. Domestic political pressure became even more acute after Yeltsin was criticized for yielding to the United States regarding the supply of missile technology to India in 1993. When U.S. pressure over Moscow's sales to Iran intensified in 1995, Yeltsin was especially disinclined to back down. This view was expressed in the Russian military daily *Krasnaia Zvezda*:

> In general, it seems that the Indian option, whereby Russia agreed, under U.S. pressure, to cut back the contract to sell cryogenic engines to India, will not be repeated with the Russian–Iranian agreement. This opens up for Russia an important direction in its foreign economic policy.[36]

Cooperation with Iran has been an important issue in Russia's internal political debates. Many political groups advocate a closer rapport with Iran (and other U.S. adversaries, such as Iraq) as a means of expressing anti-Westernism. Political analyst Sergei Karaganov, when discussing the hard-core faction that espouses a revanchist policy, explicitly refers to cooperation with Iran (and Iraq) as an element of that policy.[37] Even close associates of the West such as Yeigor Gaidar support close cooperation with Iran. And the Communists have claimed that closer relations with the United States would compromise relations with Iran, drawing Russia into the confrontation with the Muslim world. Moscow's decisions about whether or not to cooperate with Iran can also have significant domestic economic ramifications. For instance, St. Petersburg, the major political base for many Russian politicians and officials (including President Vladimir Putin himself), is also home to many of the Russian industries engaging in cooperation with Iran, especially in the nuclear field. These groups include the Leningrad Metal Works, the Science and Technology Center of Microtechnology, and Izhorsky Zavod. Politicians' decisions about cooperation with Iran can be influenced by the effect canceling a major contract would have on a particular political base.

Many Russian giant conglomerates, such as Gasprom and MINATOM (Ministry of Atomic Energy), have huge stakes in continuing their cooperation with Iran. At times, especially during the Yeltsin presidency, they conducted policy initiatives without prior political approval. Moscow often publicly dismissed the agreements that were independently orchestrated between MINATOM and Iran, claiming they were not sanctioned by the Russian leadership. That was, for instance, its response to the discovery of MINATOM's declaration of intent to supply a gas centrifuge enrichment plant to Iran.[38] Mikhail Kokeyev, first deputy director of the Security and Disarmament Department of Russia's Foreign Ministry, announced that Russia does not have any state programs of cooperation with Iran in the nuclear field that "could bring [Iran] to another military level. . . . However, there are several departmental developments that [allow] dual utilization of technologies [to be] handed over to Iran." He explained that the matter of the centrifuge was not within the framework of a state agreement, but rather an initiative of a particular government department:

> Under the present situation, the striving of different Russian departments to attract funding from the outside in order to improve their situation is quite understandable.[39]

Vladimir Lukin, chairman of the Russian Duma (Parliament) Foreign Affairs Committee, commented:

> This absolutely undesirable effect is the consequence of a "diplomacy of several doors" [occurring] when the Russian Ministry of Atomic Energy, while negotiating with Iran on the sale of light-water reactors, did not consult either the president or the government of Russia . . . As a result, it looked as if we signed a deal on behalf of Russia, although in fact it was signed on behalf of a specific ministry.[40]

Nevertheless, MINATOM's chief, Viktor Mikhailov, was not dismissed for these so-called independent initiatives—revealing that they were a tacitly accepted element of Russian policy.

The supply of nuclear power reactors and technology to various countries has been a subject of debate among Russia's government ministries. The main participants in the struggle over determining appropriate Russian policy are the Ministry of Foreign Affairs and the Ministry for Atomic Energy. Other important government agencies, such as the FSB, sometimes try to influence this policy as well. Deputy Atomic Energy Minister Yevgenii Reshetnikov observed the following, in reference to potential deals with Iran and Pakistan:

> We could earn at least $1.8–$2 billion. Pakistan had repeatedly turned to us. We have the support of the Russian Economic Ministry and other agencies, but the Foreign Ministry is thwarting all our efforts. [41]

An interview with Andrei Kozyrev during his tenure as foreign minister illustrates a similar struggle among Russian agencies regarding the supply of reactors and technology to Iran:

> Russia's Foreign Ministry, based on additional instructions from the president, will insist on making all this work subject to interdepartmental expertise so that long-term Russian state interests, rather than departmental or even commercial interests, are made a priority.[42]

The supply of nuclear reactors at Bushehr was supported by interest groups from across the Russian political spectrum. Members of Russia's environmental camp were among the only people to voice opposition to this cooperation, and these individuals proved irrelevant to Russian policymaking on this issue. Alexei Yablokov, head of the Environmental Policy Center and chair of the Russian Security Council's interdepartmental commission for ecological safety, was the most vociferous opponent of Russia's nuclear cooperation with Iran. In an attempt to avert the sale of the reactors, Yablokov wrote, "It is strange that Iran, a nation with huge stocks of oil and gas, has decided to build such a dangerous facility as a nuclear power plant." Yablokov said that his commission had submitted a report to Yeltsin objecting to the nuclear contract with Iran.[43] His warning, excerpted below, appeared in *Izvestiia*:

> The Iranian millions could in the short term serve as a gulp of oxygen for our increasingly frail atomic industry. But all of Russia will have to pay for this momentary happiness of the atomic scientists. First, there are no fundamental differences between "weapons-grade" and "non–weapons–grade" plutonium and uranium. Any reactor, a light-water reactor included, produces plutonium . . . .

> Merely the dissemination among Iranian specialists of technological knowledge in the sphere of nuclear processes and the handling of fissionable materials would represent for Iran a real breakthrough in the sphere of the creation of nuclear weapons. Is it to Russia's advantage to have a strong nuclear neighbor with a very unpredictable foreign policy in proximity to its southern borders?[44]

Two scientists, V. P. Maslov and V. P. Myasnikov, responded to Yablokov's provocative article with an editorial in *Izvestiia* declaring, "We wish to state honestly that the nuclear station which Russia has contracted to build for Iran will undoubtedly lead to the creation of nuclear weapons in Iran."[45] They continued, however, by observing the poverty of Russia's nuclear scientists and asking, "Can we assume responsibility and abandon the contract? Our reply is this: No, we cannot. We can only lay bare the problem and pose it in all is unsightliness—which is what we are doing."[46] Other environmentalists, including Vladimir Kuznetsov, director of the Russian Informational and Analytic Center for Preventing Accidents in the Atomic Energy Field, also expressed opposition to the reactor deals.

Some of those who pointed out the danger of nuclear cooperation with Iran suggested a middle road: to provide the reactors, but to exert more control over them. Some members of the Scientific and Technical Center of the Russian State Committee for the Supervision of Nuclear and Radiation Safety wrote articles suggesting additional control mechanisms.[47]

Most Russian ministers and parliament members who commented on the topic condemned the U.S. sanctions on Russian companies that cooperated with Iran and U.S. threats to cut assistance to Russia and to many Russian-American joint projects. But Vladimir Lukin, International Affairs Committee chairman of the Duma lower chamber, warned that Russia should not lightly dismiss the economic implications of defying Washington. He proposed that Moscow strongly weigh the consequences of its cooperation with Iran.[48]

Throughout most of the 1990s, while he held pivotal positions in the Russian policy elite, Yevgenii Primakov played a leading role in directing Russia's policy toward Iran. According to a Russian official who deals with policy toward the Middle East, Primakov's presence and influence continue to be reflected in Russian policy toward Iran, even though his formal tenure in Russian government has ended. Most Middle East policy players in Russia were at one time Primakov's students and have remained supporters of his outlook.[49] Under Putin's presidency, Andrei Nikolayev, chairman of the State Duma Committee for Defense and ex-director of the Russian Border Service (FPS), has emerged as one of the most prominent Russian advocates for the deepening of ties and cooperation with Iran.[50] The chief of the Armed Forces General Staff, General Anatoliy Kvashnin, has also been pushing for a resumption of military cooperation between Russia and Iran.

It seems that the foreign policy process in Russia is becoming more centralized under President Putin and that more coherent policies will emerge. Moreover, the leadership styles of certain individuals in the policymaking elite seem to have influenced Russia's Iran policy. For instance, because former President Yeltsin did not have a good grasp of various ministries and organizations' dealings with Iran, he tended to make policy commitments without fully considering their implications and establishing mechanisms for their implementation. It often appeared as if Yeltsin's commitments to the United States in this regard were almost spontaneous, rather than preceded by extensive staff work. In contrast, Putin is very much aware of the extent of Russia's dealings with Iran and what their curtailment would mean. Prior to his presidency, Putin dealt personally with many Iranian officials and with important aspects of Russia's policy. When he was head of FSB, he chose to meet with senior Iranian representatives on several occasions, demonstrating a noteworthy personal involvement and understanding in many facets of the countries' relationship.

In June 1999, Putin met with the Iranian interior minister Abdol Vahid Musavi-Lari in Moscow. It is intriguing to note Putin's remark that, despite U.S. pressure, Moscow was "committed to abide by agreements it has entered with the Islamic Republic of Iran." Putin also spoke about many regional issues, such as the countries' joint positions on Kosovo.

These statements dealt with areas far beyond the usual mandate of an FSB director, and they show that Putin was involved in high-level Russian policy toward Iran before his presidency. Putin viewed Iranian cooperation as integral to addressing the issues for which he was accountable, including threats to internal security. Perhaps the aim of the meeting between Putin and Musavi-Lari, which took place just a couple weeks before Moscow's military assault on Chechnya, was to ensure Iranian acquiescence in a planned Russian military operation. This understanding between Moscow and Tehran helped to prevent anti-Russian backlash in the Muslim world. Putin's statements about nuclear cooperation could be interpreted as assurances to the Iranians on matters important to Tehran—a grateful response to Iran for helping ensure successful results on certain issues, such as security in the northern Caucasus.

Hasan Hojjat ol-Eslam Ruhani, the secretary of the Iranian Supreme National Security Council, has played a principal role in Iran's policy and cooperation with Russia and in the Russian–Iranian roundtable forum. He is a leading advocate of close ties with Moscow. Considered a fervent hardliner within Iran, Ruhani is under frequent attack from the reformist elements who have targeted him in their efforts to remove officials. He may be removed if the reformists gain strength, and that could have a significant bearing on Russian–Iranian relations. Ruhani's removal would signify an important reformist success in the sphere of foreign policy, where that faction's influence has thus far not been considerable. Among the professional diplomats in Iran, Mahmud Va'ezi has played a prominent role in Iran's policy toward Russia as well as Central Asia and the Caucasus.

Notes

1. See for instance, Robert Rossow Jr., "The Battle of Azerbaijan, 1946," *Middle East Journal 10* (winter 1956), pp. 17-32; and Richard W. Cottam, *Nationalism in Iran: Updated Through 1978* (Pittsburgh: University of Pittsburgh Press, 1979), p. 118.

2. Many middle-class merchants, however, moved to Tehran in this period, evidently due to the consequences of the severance of economic ties with the center, where their major business partners were.

3. Ervand Abrahamian, *Iran Between Two Revolutions* (Princeton: Princeton University Press, 1982), p. 399.

4. Articles 5 and 6 of the treaty state that the USSR has the right to send troops to Iran should a third party intervene militarily there or use Iranian territory as a base for an attack on Soviet territory.

5. For example, the Vice-Speaker of the Iranian Majlis and Chair of the Iranian Supreme National Security Council, Hasan Ruhani referred to the 1921 treaty as the legal basis for the status of the Caspian Sea. Islamic Republic News Agency (IRNA), January 13, 2000; Iran's ambassador to Russia, Mehdi Safari, referred to the 1921 and 1940 treaties as a basis for the demarcation of the Caspian Sea until the concluding of a new agreement on September 27, 1999. See also *Resalat,* February 15, 1998, p. 16.

6. Galia Golan, *Soviet Polices in the Middle East: From World War II to* Gorbachev (Cambridge: Cambridge University Press, 1990), p. 184.

7. Ibid., p. 179.

8. Proceedings of the Twenty-Sixth Communist Party of the Soviet Union (CPSU) Congress.

9. Interview with Viktor Mikhailov in *Priroda*, August 1995, no. 8, pp. 3-11 (FBIS-SOV-95-245-S); *Tehran Times,* May 9, 1995, p. 1.

10. *Ettela'at,* June 28, 1989, p. 4 (FBIS-NES-89-141).

11. Ralph A. Cossa, *Iran: Soviet Interests, U.S. Concerns* (Washington, D.C.: National Defense University, Institute for National Strategic Studies, 1990), p. 81.

12. See, for instance, *Ettela'at,* February 6, 1990, p. 12.

13. IRNA in English, December 9, 1991.

14. *Tehran Times,* August 18, 1991, p. 2.

15. Statement of Deputy Foreign Minister 'Ali Mohammad Besharati, in *Abrar,* December 2, 1991, p. 2 (FBIS-NES-91-237); *Tehran Times,* December 30, 1991, p. 2.

16. *Jomhuri-ye Islami,* March 4, 1992, p. 4.

17. *Izvestiia,* April 1, 1993, p. 3 (FBIS-SOV-93-061). See also, *Izvestiia,* February 5, 1992, p. 5; Radio Moscow in Persian, October 25, 1993 (FBIS-SOV-93-207); *Izvestiia,* March 14, 2001.

18. The Soviet Union also had a similar approach to the Islamic Republic in its early days. Moscow tended to blame the anti-Soviet policies and statements from Tehran on "reactionary elements" and not on the regime itself.

19. *Tehran Times,* December 6, 1999.

20. Interfax in English, December 25, 1999.

21. For instance, see Interfax in English, December 25, 1996; Itar-Tass in English, March 3, 1998.

22. Itar-Tass, January 15, 1996.

23. *Izvestiia*, March 6, 1993; *Kommersant-Daily*, May 11, 1995, p. 1.

24. *Izvestiia*, May 7, 1996, p. 3 (FBIS-SOV-96-091).

25. Viktor Vishniakov, "Russian–Iranian Relations and Regional Stability," *International Affairs* 45, no. 1, p. 150.

26. *Rossiiskaia Gazeta*, September 22, 1994, pp. 1, 6 (FBIS-SOV-94-185).

27. *Abrar*, July 16, 1996, p. 12 (FBIS-NES-96-141).

28. *Tehran Times*, June 25, 1989, pp. 2, 3 (FBIS-NES-89-141); Shahram Chubin, *Iran's National Security Policy: Capabilities, Intentions and Impact* (Washington, D.C.: Carnegie Endowment for International Peace, 1994); and colleague's conversation with senior Iranian economist, September 2000.

29. Abbas Maleki, "The Prospects of Irano-Russian Relations," *Amu Darya* 1, no. 2 (Summer and Fall, 1996), p. 193.

30. *Salam*, May 21, 1996, p. 12 (FBIS-NES-96-106).

31. Maleki, pp. 193-194.

32. Kamal Kharrazi, "New Dimensions of Iran's Strategic Significance: Challenges, Opportunities, and Achievements," *Harvard Middle Eastern and Islamic Review* I, no. 2, p. 82.

33. There is extensive literature on factionalism and its influence on the Iranian policy formation process. See Bahman Baktiari, *Parliamentary Politics in Revolutionary Iran: The Institutionalization of Factional Politics* (Gainesville: University Press of Florida, 1996).

34. For example, *Jomhuri-ye Islami*, August 11, 1992, p. 16 (FBIS-NES-92-175); *Salam*, July 19, 1993, p. 12 (FBIS-NES-93-147). For criticism on the Iranian Foreign Ministry's policy on Chechnya, see *Jomhuri-ye Islami*, November 14, 1999, pp. 1, 2, 14 (FBIS-NES-1999-1221), *Jomhuri-ye Islami*, October 9, 1999, p. 12 (FBIS-NES-1999-1201).

35. *Kommersant-Daily*, April 22, 1995, p. 5.

36. *Krasnaia Zvezda*, April 13, 1995, p. 3 (FBIS-SOV-95-071).

37. *Moskovskiie Novosti*, February 29–March 6, 2000, pp. 5, 11 (FBIS-SOV-2000-0308).

38. See the discussion of security cooperation in Chapter 3.

39. Interfax, May 11, 1995.

40. Interfax in English, May 16, 1995.

41. Interview with Yevgenii Reshetnikov, *Moskovskiie Novosti,* no. 17, March 12–19, 1995, p. 12 (FBIS- SOV-95-053).

42. Interfax in English, April 4, 1995.

43. Interfax in English, April 15, 1996.

44. *Izvestiia,* April 12, 1995, p. 3 (FBIS-SOV-95-079).

45. *Izvestiia,* April 18, 1995, p. 3 (FBIS-SOV-95-074).

46. Ibid.

47. *Izvestiia* (Financial section), June 15, 1995, p. iv.

48. Itar-Tass in English, January 14, 1999.

49. Interview with the author, winter 2000.

50. *Tehran Times,* November 26, 2000.

Chapter 3

Relations between Russia and Iran

"Iran is Russia's neighbor and Russia has to cooperate with it." —*Oleg Davidov, Russian minister for foreign economic relations, May 1995*

Since the early 1990s, Russia and Iran have each viewed their mutual cooperation as an important element of national security. By 1993, senior officials from each side referred to these relations on a regular basis as "strategic," and the intensity of the two countries' cooperation reflected this status. During a visit to Moscow in March 1996, Iranian foreign minister 'Ali Akbar Velayati stated that Iranian–Russian relations were "at their highest level in contemporary history."[1] The cooperation between Tehran and Moscow was driven by a number of factors, including geographic proximity; the perception of compatible interests in a number of regional zones (Central Asia, the Caucasus, and the Middle East); both countries' political isolation; the compatibility of one country being a major arms producer and the other being an important consumer; and the mutual perception of a need to combat the emerging unipolar system of U.S. hegemony.

Observers often overlook the importance of the geographic factor in the relations between Iran and Russia. Good relations and cooperation are a crucial element of national security for the two neighbors—certainly they are more than a luxury or merely an opportunity for a foreign policy gain. Writing about the Russian point of view, First Deputy Chairman of the Russian State Duma Mikhail Mityukov observed:

> The geopolitical aspect is important—if Iran, a country [far away] from the United States, causes inconveniences for it,

29

why should Russia face similar problems with Iran, its neighbor?[2]

Close relations and cooperation between Russia and Iran complement a number of their respective interests. In the spring of 1998, Vitaliy Naumkin observed:

Russia actively develops both economic and political relations with Iran. Politically, [this relationship] can balance Russian relations with the West; help to contain other regional powers; neutralize possible attempts of Iran itself to dominate Central Asia (or at least some of its regions); allow Moscow to retain and even extend its influence in the Middle East; deprive the anti-Yeltsin opposition of the trump card of accusing the government of a pro-Western bias;[3] and strengthen its positions in the solution of the problem of the legal status of the Caspian Sea.[4]

Iranian politicians also appreciate the advantages they derive from relations with Russia. The Islamic Republic News Agency (IRNA) reported that Iranian foreign minister Kamal Kharrazi, in talks with Russian foreign minister Igor Ivanov, stressed the many Iranian interests served by close cooperation with Russia:

Referring to the effective cooperation between the two countries in settling regional issues such as peace in Tajikistan, [Iranian president Mohammad] Khatami stressed the necessity of Tehran–Moscow cooperation to put an end to clashes in Afghanistan and set up a government there based on sustainable peace that would be beneficial to all groups. He further pointed to the joint views of the two countries in opposing a unipolar world and noted that the demographic, historical, and cultural structure as well as the vast potentials of Iran and Russia allowed them to play a decisive role in creating a multipolar system. Stating that the Caucasus is so important both to Iran and Russia that the national security of the two countries is affected by the region's peace and security, Khatami said alien powers whose interests are not in the same line as those of regional peoples and countries should not be permitted to intervene and penetrate into the Caucasus.[5]

Russia and Iran established a number of forums and commissions for regular exchanges, in an attempt to institutionalize the cooperation between them. One such commission is the Russian–Iranian Roundtable. The Russian delegation is headed by Vitaliy Naumkin, and at the latest meeting the Iranian delegation was chaired by Seyyed Kharrazi, Iranian undersecretary for education and research at the Ministry of Foreign Affairs. Iran's Institute for Political and International Studies (IPIS) and the Russian Institute for Strategic and International Studies (RISIS) sponsor the roundtable. In addition, the two sides established a Permanent Russian–Iranian Intergovernmental Commission for Economic Cooperation in 1996, headed by the vice premier of the Russian government and Iran's minister of the economy and finances. The heads of the various security services and organs meet frequently for consultation, and regular cooperation has been instituted between the two states' national security councils.

The style in which Russian and Iranian officials treat each other plays an important role in fostering the relations between them. While Russians are frequently sidelined in Western capitals and treated as poor and powerless, in Tehran they are treated as representatives of an important country. Iranian officials, similarly, are treated as emissaries of a significant state when they are in Moscow.

Both sides are committed to maintaining a stable border zone in the region they share, and their mutual cooperation is essential to achieving this common goal. As Naumkin explains:

> Russia regards the maintenance of friendly relations with the countries bordering on the Commonwealth of Independent States (CIS) as one of the important trends in its foreign policy. Among these countries, Iran, as a major regional power, having a substantial influence on the situa-

tion in Central Asia and Transcaucasia, occupies one of the first places.[6]

Their relations and cooperation in a number of fields are interconnected. For instance, their collaboration on nuclear issues affects their domestic agendas, as each country sees the other as important to ensuring its internal stability and territorial integrity. According to Naumkin:

> In Iran, apprehensions are expressed concerning the future of the Russian federal state, arising, above all, from the bitter experience of the Chechen conflict. Yet, one should dare to say that Russia is not threatened by a breakup, and the centrifugal inertia will be overcome. But the above-mentioned challenges do exist both for Russia (although Russians make up more than 80 percent of the country's population) and for Iran (where ethnic Persians total probably a little more than 50 percent of the population).[7]

Moscow's vulnerability in Chechnya is pivotal to understanding the extent of its commitment to cooperate with Iran in a variety of fields. Russia needs Iran to contain foreign Muslim influence over Chechnya and to prevent Muslim criticism of Moscow. Similarly, Iran views Russia as a partner in checking Azerbaijan's progress. A weak Azerbaijan is not in a position to incite the Azerbaijani population in Iran. According to the Iranian newspaper *Abrar:*

> Iran's significance is so great that Moscow believes that cooperating with it could—in addition to cutting the United States' hands off short of the Caucasus and Central Asia—prevent external influences from breaking up the northern Caucasus and the other Muslim-inhabited areas in Russia.[8]

Once the two countries established regular cooperation in the second half of 1993, subsequent disagreements in the regional sphere rarely had a negative effect on their bilateral cooperation. Even when Tehran expressed some limited criticism of Moscow's policies (such as in Chechnya), that criticism remained rhetorical and did not diminish the practical coop-eration between the two countries. Rather, military and other delegations continued this cooperation throughout the Rus-sian assaults on Chechnya.

Russian pledges to cooperate with Iran in the nuclear and security fields seemed to surge during Russia's heightened military engagements in Chechnya. In January 1995, while Iranian media sources published criticisms of Russia's actions in Chechnya and students demonstrated in front of the Rus-sian embassy in Tehran, Viktor Mikhailov, the Russian minister of atomic energy, arrived in Tehran to "conclude a contract on completion and putting into operation of the Atomic Energy Plant project."[9] In addition, while Moscow was inten-sively bombing Chechnya in January 2000, the head of the Iranian Supreme Council of National Security, Hasan Ruhani, visited Moscow. There he met with Russian defense minister Igor Sergeyev, who pledged to maintain military ties between Russia and Iran.[10]

At the beginning of the Russian assault on Chechnya in the autumn of 1999, Iran's ambassador to Russia, Mehdi Sa-fari, stated that Iran and Russia should develop cooperation in all spheres, including the military and technical realms.[11] The Moscow daily *Izvestiia* reported in January 2000 that Rus-sia had resumed its weapons sales to Iran, and linked the change to the Chechnya issue—implying that it signified a payoff to Iran for quelling Muslim criticism of Russia's ac-tions.[12] Moreover, at the historic December 2000 visit of Sergeyev to Iran—during which Russian arms supplies to Iran occupied a major part of the discussions—the head of the Russian Defense Ministry's Main Directorate for International Military Cooperation, General-Colonel Leonid Ivashov, stated that the Russian delegation "noted with satisfaction that the Iranian position on events in Chechnya was fairly restrained."[13]

At the same time, Moscow has conducted a misinforma-tion campaign about many of the national and other dissident movements in Central Asia, the Caucasus, and the Muslim-populated areas of Russia. This policy had a dual purpose. First, Russia cast aspersions on these movements by exaggerating the extent of their threat and linking them to other movements (such as the Taliban) already feared by the Russian population, in order to mobilize support for actions against them. Second, Russia sought to foster Western support for its actions against these movements by painting a picture of common interests between Moscow and Washington in countering "the Islamic threat."

Moscow immediately implicated Chechens in a number of deadly explosions in Russia during the second half of 1999. However, Russian officials never presented evidence that convincingly linked the Chechen national movement with this series of bombings. Russia has a clear interest in presenting evidence that attests to Chechen complicity; surely, if it had convincing proof, it would reveal it. The fact that it has blamed the Chechen national movement without proof illustrates the political motives behind attributing these acts to the Chechens. Moreover, Moscow often linked Osama bin Ladin to events in Chechnya as a means of fostering U.S. sympathy for Russian actions there, without bringing significant evidence to illustrate such a link.

The pattern of erroneously attributing political disturbances involving Muslims to "Islam" emerged prior to the Soviet breakup. When Uzbek Muslims clashed with fellow Muslim Meshketians in the Fergana Valley of Uzbekistan in 1989, Soviet leader Mikhail Gorbachev blamed the incidents on Islamic fundamentalism and remarked that "Islam had exposed its fangs." In addition, when Azerbaijanis in Soviet Azerbaijan attempted to tear down border posts and meet their co-ethnics in the Azerbaijani-populated provinces of Iran in January 1990, Gorbachev blasted the Azerbaijanis for supposedly turning to Khomeinism on the eve of the massive introduction of Soviet troops in Baku. During the post-Soviet period, Russia has continued this policy of characterizing challenges from nominally Muslims groups as "Islamic threats," especially in the case of the Chechen struggle.

The United States views Tehran as a major source and proponent of Islamic-based violence, and in the early 1990s many Washington policymakers expected that Russia would share the United States' interests in combating terror. They assumed that Moscow would perceive a threat emerging from Iran, especially in light of the Chechen challenge. But Moscow's actual stance on Islamic terror is much more complicated. First, it seems that Russian policymakers actually view the danger as far more modest than their rhetorically exaggerated statements suggest. Second, Russia believes that the most significant Islamic-based threats to its security emanate from nonstate-supported groups in Western–oriented states such as Saudi Arabia, Pakistan, and Turkey, and it blames the United States for arming and training the Afghan rebel groups that today serve as a chief source of Islamic-based terror. Thus, Moscow does not share the U.S. view that the two countries possess common interests in combating Islamic threats, especially with regard to Iran.

Russia's cooperation with Iran in defiance of strong U.S. objections is facilitated by the fact that close U.S. allies such as Japan and most Western European states also conduct cooperation and trade with Tehran. Moreover, as was discussed above, even those Russians who postulate that Tehran is a major source of Islamic agitation in Central Asia and the Caucasus claim that the best remedy is cooperation with Iran. Moscow believes that frequent contacts with Tehran give it more leverage to prevent Iranian-sponsored support for Islamic groups in the region. Russia also seems to support Iran's association with groups in Central Asia and the Caucasus that engage in political Islam, as a way to co-opt and partially control them. If Iran has some influence over these groups, Russia can make arrangements with them as well.

One snag in the relationship between Iran and Russia, however, has been the lack of serious trade between them. Tehran's poor payment record has especially impeded economic relations, as Naumkin describes:

> Russian–Iranian trade and economic relations have been hampered by a number of difficulties, including the non-

observance by the Iranian side of the dates and terms of payments. Some of the agreements remain on paper, or their realization proceeds with an appreciable delay.[14]

Preventing U.S. Hegemony

Moscow and Tehran's bilateral ties serve an important role in advancing aspects of their respective international agendas. Both are interested in preventing "U.S. hegemony" and the emergence of a "monolithic international system," and this shared goal has played an important role in cementing their relations. They see their mutual cooperation as a means of countering U.S. supremacy and U.S. attempts to sideline each of them.

Furthermore, through their common relations, Iran and Russia both gain more maneuverability in deflecting regional and even international challenges. Tehran and Moscow are further united by their mutual opposition to the expansion of the North Atlantic Treaty Organization (NATO) to include the states of the former Soviet Union and their desire to limit the U.S. presence in the Caspian region. Moscow's relations with Iran (and other "outsiders," such as Iraq) endow Russia with a unique role in the international system, contributing to its claim to great-power status. By way of its relations with Iran and other states, Russia retains some leverage over the United States and some means of deterring what it views as the U.S. diktat. A commentator in the Russian newspaper *Segodnia* wrote the following on the importance of Russia's relations with Iran: "Since Russia could conclude military alliances with other anti-Western fundamentalist regimes as well, even a weak Russia can, theoretically, oppose the last remaining superpower."[15]

Moscow's commitment to challenge U.S. hegemony in the international system increased in the year 2000, following President Vladimir Putin's election. This was articulated in Russia's official foreign policy doctrine, published in February of that year. Moscow's relations with Iran play a role in this attempt at changing the balance of forces.

Despite their common interests with regard to the United States, however, both Moscow and Tehran recognize that a change in U.S.–Iranian relations could greatly affect Russian–Iranian relations. Moscow views Iran's seclusion as an asset, as the following commentator notes:

> It seems that failing to take advantage of Iran's relative isolation and passing up the possibility to enhance Russia's economic and technological potential . . . with the aid of Iran's promising market would be not only a big economic mistake but also a political mistake.[16]

A number of Russian officials have remarked that, in spite of Moscow's official rhetoric calling for a renewal of ties between the United States and Iran, Moscow actually stands to lose a lot of ground from such a rapprochement and will actively work to thwart it.

Russia's Assertion of an Independent Foreign Policy

Moscow's relations with Iran symbolize an independent Russian foreign policy that defies U.S. interests. As was discussed in Chapter One, Russia's relations with Iran have become intertwined with internal political struggles regarding the extent to which Moscow should cooperate and align itself with Washington's policies. In 1993, the Russian ambassador to Iran pointed out, "We consider our relations with Iran an element of our independent foreign policy."[17]

On the heels of what were perceived to be a number of Russian concessions to Washington in the foreign policy domain, Washington began an intensive effort to prevent Russian–Iranian cooperation in fields that could advance Iran's nonconventional weapons program.[18] With these previous concessions in mind, many forces in Moscow hardened their position on Iran, which they viewed as an especially important partner and potential client.

Regional Interests

Moscow and Tehran perceive themselves as possessing a number of common interests in the region they both border—Central Asia and the Caucasus—as well as a limited number of shared interests in the Middle East. In regions where they once supported rival factions, such as Tajikistan, they have frequently concluded that it is preferable to cooperate and overcome their differences in an attempt to prevent the United States or other countries from taking a leading role in negotiations or security arrangements. Hasan Ruhani, chair of the Iranian National Security Council, stated:

> In view of the fact that the United States is planning to extend its influence in the Caucasus and Central Asian regions, Iranian and Russian statesmen have taken effective steps during the recent years aimed at consolidating mutual ties for confronting Washington's interventionist polices. On this basis, Tehran and Moscow have helped to settle regional disputes, including the Tajik and Afghan crisis. For both states are well aware of the fact that the regional crisis can facilitate U.S. intervention in the region. Iran and Russia's success in helping to end the Tajik crisis via political means is a good example.[19]

Moreover, in areas such as the Balkans where their interests or partners occasionally clashed, Iran and Russia have tended in public statements to declare that they share common interests, reinforcing the importance that both countries attach to their bilateral relationship.

Central Asia and the Caucasus

Russia and Iran's respective approaches to Central Asia have gone through a number of evolutions since the Soviet breakup. Even during the initial stages, when the sides differed sharply over a number of regional issues (such as Tajikistan and Nagorno–Karabagh), both labored to ensure that disagreements in regional arenas would not project negatively onto their bilateral relationship or derail other forms of cooperation.

In the second half of 1993, Iran and Russia recognized the importance of their bilateral relations and chose to forgo competition with one another for control over negotiations and security arrangements in the region. By late 1993, conflicts in Central Asia and the Caucasus had escalated to a point that alarmed both Moscow and Tehran and called for containment measures to prevent regional spillover. Their assessment of common interests in the region contrasts with the initial U.S. assumption following the Soviet collapse that Russia and Iran were competitors in Central Asia and that this competition would emerge as a source of tension in Russian–Iranian relations.

Russian–Iranian cooperation was facilitated by changes that emerged in their respective policies toward the overall region. Russia's policy toward Central Asia and the Caucasus has evolved significantly since the Soviet breakup. From the collapse of the USSR until about 1994, Moscow engaged in an aggressive policy aimed at returning Russian troops to many of the former borders of the USSR and retaining domination over economic and strategic developments in the region. Moscow's regional policy was not highly centralized in this period, and various arms of the government, from the Ministry of Defense to individual commanders in the field, often independently carried out policies that they interpreted as promoting Russia's best interests. In its attempt to gain influence over the region, Moscow often relied on the assistance of local dissident groups (such as the rebels in the Abkhaz region of the Republic of Georgia), which had a very destabilizing effect on the Caucasus in the early 1990s.

From the 1990s onward, Moscow's policy toward Central Asia and the Caucasus went through a significant transformation. First, Russia's goals in the region became progressively more modest. Central control over various government organs was enhanced and policy became more coordinated, especially since Putin assumed office. Finally, since the Chechen conflict, Russia has come to realize the long-term danger inherent in its policy of positioning different forces in the region against each other. Although Moscow still strives to maintain influence in and obtain benefits from the region, the means it chooses to implement these goals seem to have changed.

Iran's foreign policy toward Central Asia is predominantly guided by geopolitical state interests; ideological goals, such as the promotion of Islam, have secondary importance. In contrast, prior to the Soviet collapse, Tehran was more supportive of Islamic movements and Muslim peoples in the region because the risks involved in taking such a stance were not as significant. With the collapse of the Soviet Union, however, Iran grasped the fact that a potentially conflict-laden zone had replaced its once stable northern border, and that influences from the new states could quickly permeate through Iran.

Following the Soviet breakup, Tehran took a very sober attitude toward the establishment of the new Muslim republics. It saw in this development the dangers that could emanate from internal ethnic factors within Iran, as well as possible opportunities to enjoy expanded influence in the region. In late 1991, a commentator in the *Tehran Times* explained that

> The first ground for concern from the point of view in Tehran is the lack of political stability in the newly independent republics. The unstable conditions in those republics could be serious causes of insecurity along the lengthy borders (more than 2,000 kilometers) Iran shares with those countries. Already foreign hands can be felt at work in those republics, especially in Azerbaijan and Turkmenistan . . . with the ultimate objective of brewing discord among the Iranian Azeris and Turkmen by instigating ethnic and nationalistic sentiments.[20]

On the policy level, when geopolitical interests conflict with commitments of "Islamic solidarity" in Central Asia, Tehran almost always gives preference to the geopolitical considerations. Moreover, Iran generally advances the propagation of Islam and supports Islamic elements in a way that does not hurt its bilateral state interests in Central Asia, and it has promoted these causes most intensively in areas not contiguous to Iran (such as Tajikistan and Uzbekistan) where there is little risk of a spillover of destabilizing activity.

In the early 1990s, Iran was active in giving direct aid to the Islamic-oriented section of the Tajik opposition (the Islamic Renaissance Party). This assistance declined significantly after 1993, a development that facilitated the emergence of greater cooperation between Tehran and Moscow in the region. At times, Tehran has given or withheld aid to Islamic elements in Central Asian and Caucasus states as a way of applying pressure on the states in the region. Consequently, it is difficult to say in these cases whether the propagation of Islam abroad is ideologically motivated or if it is an instrument used to advance state interests. [21] The latter scenario is often the case in relations with Azerbaijan, where Iran has at times given support to subversive Islamic elements as a means to pressure Baku on various policies.

One of the primary goals of Tehran's policies in Central Asia and the Caucasus is to prevent events in the region from influencing Iran's own ethnic minorities. As indicated above, Iran is a multi-ethnic society in which 50 percent of the citizens are of non-Persian origin. Tehran's policy considerations are especially problematic because of the regime's sometimes conflicting goals. For example, Iran cooperated with Armenia during the Nagorno–Karabagh War in order to ensure that Azerbaijan did not become a source of attraction for Iran's Azerbaijani community; but this policy conflicted with Iran's other security goals, such as maintaining a stable border area.

One of the factors that cements Iran and Russia together in Central Asia and the Caucasus is their shared interest in preventing the expansion of U.S. and Turkish presence and influence in the area.[22] Tehran desires a Russian presence as a bulwark against the United States. In the summer of 1995, Mohammed Reza Bakhtiyari, director-general of the Iranian Foreign Ministry responsible for Central Asia and the Caucasus affirmed, "We believe that Russia's presence in Central Asia and the Caucasus is necessary."[23] At the same time, Iran prefers that armed forces from the former Soviet republics, rather than Russian troops, be stationed on the borders that Iran shares with the states of that region.[24]

Chechnya

Russia's belief that it needs Iran as a partner in containing potential Islamic-based threats is illustrated by the two countries' interactions concerning Chechnya. For Russia, it is critical that Iran refrain from strongly criticizing Moscow's policies in Chechnya or from providing major support to the Chechens; otherwise a general Muslim campaign could be launched against Russia.

Iran's reactions to both the first and second Chechen conflicts in the 1990s illustrate the nonideological nature of its policy toward the Caucasus and the importance it assigns to its relations with Russia. Considering the Muslim background of the Chechen rebels, the Iranian government and media were quite mild in their criticism of Russia's conduct in these wars. Tehran has been willing to play a major role in preventing Muslim criticism of Russia, and Moscow has rewarded Tehran for this role. In response to the first Chechen conflict, Russian interior minister Anatoliy Kuliko thanked Iran for keeping the Chechnya issue off the agenda at the summit of the Islamic Conference Organization. Interfax reported:

> At meetings with Iran's First Vice President Hassan Habibi and Interior Minister 'Abdollah Nuri-Hoseynabadi, Kuliko expressed gratitude to Tehran for its "circumspect position on the Chechen issue." It was Iran's stance, the Russian minister said, that prevented Turkey from putting the matter on the agenda for the final day of the Tehran summit.[25]

Iranian officials frequently commented that the Chechen conflict was an internal Russian matter and were careful not to take any steps that they thought might harm Tehran's relations with Moscow. In the context of Chechnya, Iranian officials and government media organs have even emphasized their support for the preservation of the territorial integrity of Russia. In response to the first Chechen conflict, IRNA reported that

The Iranian ambassador stressed that Iran believe[s] in the territorial integrity of Russia, and that Iran considers the problem in Chechnya as being an internal problem, and it fully supports a peaceful settlement of the situation in that republic.[26]

In reporting on a meeting between Putin and Iranian foreign minister Kamal Kharrazi in November 1999 to discuss the Chechen conflict, the Tehran-based Voice of the Islamic Republic of Iran reported that "Iran attaches much significance to the preservation of stability and security as well as the territorial integrity of Russia."[27] IRNA attributed similar statements of support for Russian territorial integrity to Iranian president Khatami.[28] At the height of the Russian actions against the Chechens, Kharrazi contributed to Moscow's media campaign dealing with the Chechen war by signing an agreement with Russian foreign minister Igor Ivanov pledging their common commitment to the preservation of human rights.[29]

In contrast, Iranian hardliner elements often expressed critical views of Moscow's actions in Chechnya in their organs of the Iranian media, such as the newspaper *Jomhuri-ye Islami*. In addition, Tehran's official response to the Chechen struggle became a subject of criticism by proponents of a more Islamic-based foreign policy. According to *Jomhuri-ye Islami*, "The fact that the foreign affairs minister has interpreted the outrageous tragedies in Chechnya, and the genocide of Muslims, as an 'internal issue,' will never be acceptable."[30]

In their criticism of the Iranian Foreign Ministry, however, Iranian hardliners occasionally took unexpected tacks. For instance, *Kayhan International* published a number of articles that were highly critical of Russia.[31] And rather than predictably assert the need for Islamic solidarity and support for fellow Muslims, an article in *Jomhuri-ye Islami* suggested that Tehran's inaction on the Chechen front hurt its own image in the world scene:

Unfortunately, either because of our silence, or some incorrect statements by some of the officials from our Foreign Affairs Ministry, the foreign media are broadcasting news to the rest of the world that Islamic Iran is standing alongside Russia with regard to the war in Chechnya. This claim is very unpleasant for the Islamic Republic of Iran. In this great war, the diplomatic authorities of the Islamic Republic of Iran should not speak in such a way that international public opinion may conclude Iran is standing alongside Russia in this war. *Although we do not expect Islamic Iran to position itself alongside the resistance of the Caucasian Muslims,* we should not act in a way that benefits the Russians by suppressing the Caucasian Muslims. This would be a heavy blow to the credibility of [an] Islamic Iran that supports the revolutionary Muslims of the world. Hopefully, the officials of the Iranian Foreign Affairs Ministry will pay more attention in this regard.[32]

Iran's criticisms of Russia's role in Chechnya were often tempered by Tehran's claims that the United States (and sometimes Israel) were responsible for Moscow's policies.[33] The Voice of the Islamic Republic of Iran reported, "The main scenarist behind this crisis is the United States, thanks to the collapse of its old rival."[34] The Iranian daily *Ettela'at* reported that "most political observers believe that with its overt and covert assistance to Russia in massacring the Chechen Muslims, the United States is seeking to tarnish Russia's image before Iran in this manner."[35]

Iranian criticisms of Russia were confined to the rhetorical level, and concrete cooperation between the two countries was never disrupted by disagreements over Chechnya. In fact, at the height of Moscow's actions in Chechnya, Iranian and Russian delegations often held meetings on furthering their cooperation, even in the military sphere. Furthermore, Moscow often rewarded Iran's compliance on the Chechen issue with public reaffirmations of its commitment to supply Tehran with much sought-after nuclear reactors.[36] For example, during the first Chechen war, Minister of Atomic Energy Viktor Mikhailov visited Tehran and met with representatives of the Iranian Atomic Energy Organization to renew the construction of the Bushehr nuclear power plant.

In addition, in September 1999, at the apex of Moscow's autumn assaults on the Chechens, Russia announced that it has signed a $38 million contract to provide a necessary turbine to the Bushehr plant.[37] At that time, Moscow also thanked Tehran for its assistance in explaining Russian actions in Chechnya to the larger community of Islamic countries: "Moscow attaches great significance to the efforts of Iran as chairman of the Islamic Conference Organization to explain the developments in Dagestan to the Islamic world."[38] Thanks to these efforts, the Russian foreign ministry acknowledged, the Islamic Conference Organization's member-countries hold "a sufficiently balanced and favorable attitude to the actions of the Russian leadership in the North Caucasus."[39]

Even Iranian journals that published articles that were critical of Russia's actions in Chechnya often pointed out that this issue should not damage bilateral cooperation between Moscow and Tehran. In response to the December 1999 announcement of the agreement to build the Baku–Ceyhan Caspian pipeline according to Washington's wishes, the following remarks appeared in *Kayhan International*:

> The Caspian is a typical example of how common interests make it necessary for Iran and Russia to join hands for the protection of their interests and those of the region. Political observers believe that the United States is following two major political objectives in the region: seeking to weaken Iran and Russia and to undermine their interests; and seeking to strengthen Turkey and Israel and to try to promote their interests. Such developments, together with many other vital bilateral and regional issues, push Iran and Russia toward greater cooperation for the sake of their national interests.[40]

Some Iranian media sources went so far as to describe the Chechen fighters as "terrorizing secessionists" when calling for Moscow to differentiate between them and the general Chechen population.[41] At the height of the 1999 Russian campaign in Chechnya, Foreign Minister Kharrazi once again termed Iran's relations with Russia as "strategic" and called for an "expansion of these ties."[42]

Iran's generally mild response to Russia's actions in Chechnya was reinforced by the Chechen rebels' attempts to receive support and recognition from the Taliban. Iran views the Taliban as extremely threatening and feels theologically justified in not supporting groups associated with it. Moreover, Tehran is aware that the Chechens have sought ties with the West. In January 2000, one commentator in the Iranian newspaper *Asr-e Ma* argued that there is no anti-Western theme within the rhetoric or goals of the mainstream elements among the Chechens, and thus their struggle does not advance Tehran's geopolitical interests:

> The last link in the chain of American efforts for weakening Russia (the heir to the former Soviet Union) is to bring about the disintegration of the Russian Federation that is made up of more than a score of autonomous republics. Meanwhile, the weakest link in the chain of the countries that provides—due to economic problems, lack of development, and religious and ethnic differences—the greatest opportunity [for America] is Chechnya, which has had a long history of clashes [against Russia]. In view of these considerations, the Chechen conflict with Russia [has] received the support of the West, especially that of the United States.
>
> When at the height of the clashes the Chechen government asks America and Israel to intervene and to support it, this provides a clear sign of the existence of such a link [between American policies and the clashes]. When the Chechen government is recognized by the regime of the Taliban that has its own problem of legitimacy in the world, one should look for the roots of this recognition in the above scenario. Therefore, those who advocate that our foreign policy must support the Chechen fighters and the Muslim government of Chechnya must think harder about the disintegration of Russia, instability in the Caucasus, and American and Israeli intervention in the region.[43]

South Caucasus

In the initial period after the Soviet breakup, Iran and Russia clashed over some of the developments in the Nagorno–

Karabagh conflict between Armenia and Azerbaijan, and their statements and policies reflected a lack of trust for each other at this time. For example, Armenian forces overtook the city of Shusha (a strategic turnabout and a major escalation of the conflict) in May 1992, when Tehran was hosting a summit of the leaders of Azerbaijan and Armenia. Iran interpreted this attack as a Russian-sponsored effort to undermine Iran's leadership role in the Caucasus. Later in the first half of the decade, however, the two countries discovered many common interests in this conflict, and that discovery contributed to the cementing of their cooperation in the Caucasus.

Russia used the conflict as a means to increase the military dependency of Yerevan on Moscow and to elicit concessions from Baku, especially in the security domain. Both Iran and Russia shared an interest in keeping Azerbaijan bogged down in a conflict and unable to carry out its plans for Western-led economic development and the transport of Caspian oil. Moreover, Iran's fear that the Republic of Azerbaijan would serve as a model for an incipient ethnic-based identity among its own Azerbaijani community led to its interest in prolonging the Nagorno–Karabagh conflict, albeit at a low level of intensity.

During the same period, cooperation between Tehran and Moscow in the Caucasus was facilitated by a shift in Russia's policy toward the region that reflected a modification of some of its goals and allowed for more accommodation of other powers. Although both Russia and Iran took advantage of the Nagorno–Karabagh conflict to advance their own regional interests, neither wanted the conflict to escalate to a degree that would cause a tremendous outpouring of refugees, which could spill over into their respective territories.

Iran's approach toward the southern Caucasus, and especially its close relations and cooperation with the Republic of Armenia, best illustrates the nonideological nature of Tehran's policy in the region. Despite its rhetoric of neutrality in the Nagorno–Karabagh conflict (a position inherently inconsistent with the official ideology of a state that portrays itself as the world's protector and champion of the Shi'i), Iran cooperated with Armenia throughout most of the post-independence period. Faced with Shi'i Azerbaijan's struggle against Armenia, Iran evidently preferred for Azerbaijan to remain besieged and unable to allocate resources to stir up Iran's Azerbaijani community to create a potential "South Azerbaijan." Tehran adopted anti-Armenian rhetoric only during the times when the results of the conflict directly threatened Iranian state interests.

Tehran's policy toward the Karabagh conflict is a good example of the diversity of opinion—the reality, in contrast with the monolithic image—evident in the foreign policymaking process in Iran. The official foreign policy establishment position was to promote quiet support for Armenia in the conflict and expanded cooperation with Yerevan, evidently as a counter to potential Azerbaijani irredentism. This policy was reflected in newspapers such as the *Tehran Times*, but it encountered open opposition from ideological stalwarts who, writing in *Jomhuri-ye Islami*, advocated Islamic solidarity toward the Azerbaijanis.

Even within the Iranian Foreign Ministry, there were diverging opinions on the conflict. Some actors, such as Deputy Foreign Minister Mahmad Va'ezi, seemed to think that there was an institutional interest in Iran's serving as a successful sponsor of the negotiation process between the conflicting sides. The fact that he candidly attempted to fulfill a positive role in the negotiations, contrary to the evolving trend of Tehran–Moscow rapprochement, indicates his apparent honesty in the negotiation process—and may not have reflected the prevailing Iranian policy. The different viewpoints of various policymakers in Iran toward the conflict and toward relations with Azerbaijan and Armenia partially explain some of the policy inconsistencies and shifts regarding Karabagh.

Caspian Sea

Russia and Iran, together with Kazakhstan, Azerbaijan, and Turkmenistan, are littoral states on the Caspian Sea, a large, landlocked body of water. The ties and cooperation between Iran and Russia received a significant boost in 1994, when

Washington articulated a policy toward the Caspian region and became more seriously involved there. Tehran and Moscow share the goals of preventing an increased U.S. and Turkish presence and influence in the Caspian region and thwarting U.S. political and corporate ambitions to lead the exploitation of the energy resources of the area. Moreover, Iran and Russia have jointly opposed the Main Export Pipeline for transporting the region's oil along an east-west (Baku–Ceyhan) route.[44]

Both Iran and Russia have made significant attempts to hinder the construction of the east-west pipeline. Their motivation is not simply the desire to gain from the tariffs that would ensue from the pipelines' traversing their territories. Instead, Russia and Iran oppose the east-west pipeline because they aspire to command the control over the flow of Caspian energy resources. Both countries are important energy producers, and their economies are fully dependent on oil incomes. Slight fluctuations in world oil prices would have significant repercussions on their economies. The expected volume of Caspian oil, although not huge, could contribute to a decrease in oil prices.[45] Moreover, Russia and Iran want to deny the states of the Caspian region the independence and political advantages that the oil revenues would provide, in order to maintain their own political control over this area that they both border.

Overall, Russia and Iran share many common interests regarding Caspian oil and gas. The division of sovereignty in the Caspian Sea is officially discussed as a legal issue, and both states have been leading the campaign aimed at thwarting development projects of the Caspian energy resources. Most of the confirmed significant findings of oil and gas are in sectors claimed by Azerbaijan, Kazakhstan, and Turkmenistan. One of the ways in which Iran and Russia have attempted to delay the development of Caspian energy resources and the Western-supported pipeline route has been through legal challenges to the other littoral states' rights to decide independently on the projects. Russia and Iran are both interested in preventing, or at least minimizing, U.S. leadership in the energy and pipeline projects; and in impeding the Caspian states' achievement of greater independence through newfound economic wealth as oil and gas producers.

Despite these common interests in the area, tensions have often emerged between Russia and Iran over the Caspian Sea, especially over the delineation of its different sectors. Until the late 1990s, Tehran and Moscow generally claimed that all the littoral states of the Caspian Sea should have joint control over the sea and its vast resources and invoked the Soviet–Iranian treaties of 1921 and 1940 to reinforce this position.[46] Iran still claims that its preferred position is one of joint sovereignty over the Caspian, but that it is willing to acquiesce to divisions of equal proportions to each littoral state. Russia's official stance on the status of the Caspian has changed a number of times since the Soviet breakup, and Iran seemed ready to alter its stance when there was an opportunity to participate in major oil projects.

Although Russia and Iran attempt to present delineation as a strictly legal issue, the recurrent shifts in their positions indicate that Russia and Iran's legal stances are tactical, but their overriding concerns are political and economic. When opportunities for involvement in certain oil and gas exploitation projects have arisen, Iran and Russia have been willing to abandon their legal stances in order to allow the energy projects to move forward. [47]

Disagreements about the Caspian's status have frequently surfaced in both the Russian and Iranian press.[48] An article that appeared in the major Iranian daily *Resalat* in 1998 noted:

> Four out of the five Caspian Sea littoral states have at least, in principle, agreed upon the kind of legal regime which this sea should have—something which can weaken the legal position of the Iranian government. Iran's position was shaped, in part, by relying on Russia's position. However, it has become unbalanced now that Russia and Turkmenistan have abandoned their positions.

This situation can only be rectified if the government abandons its current reactive position and adopts innovative policies so as to prevent Iran from becoming sidelined in the talks to determine the legal regime. The Islamic Republic of Iran should no longer consider Russia and Turkmenistan as reliable partners but as rivals who consider their national interests more important than the security and welfare of the Caspian Sea.[49]

Russia and Iran are both aware that their respective positions on the Caspian are tenuous, but because of each side's frequent policy shifts, they do not trust each other to maintain a united front on this issue. It may be a significant factor of tension between them in the future, but at this point, their overall relations have not been seriously damaged by these disagreements.

Following Putin's election to the presidency of Russia, Moscow launched a series of concerted and coherent policy initiatives aimed at raising its influence in the Caspian arena. As part of this initiative, one month after the election Putin appointed Deputy Foreign Minister Viktor Kaluzhny to serve as special presidential envoy for Caspian affairs. Kaluzhny initiated a number of proposals aimed at expanding Russia's involvement in the Caspian projects, including the resolution of the legal status of the Caspian Sea. He discussed proposals that revealed Russia's willingness to abandon the joint-control position and the alternative 20 percent division principle that it previously shared with Tehran. This action created discord with Tehran, which felt betrayed, and greater tension may emerge between the two countries. The Islamic Republic News Agency (IRNA), attributing remarks to a source in the Iranian Foreign Ministry, explained Tehran's position on the Russian initiative:

The collapse of the Soviet Union in 1991 and its division into a number of republics, with three of them bordering the [Caspian] Sea, did not have the least effect on Iran's share of the sea.

[This foreign ministry official] said that the Russian Federation as the successor of the former Soviet Union could divide its 50 percent share of the sea among the three independent littoral republics (in case the Islamic Republic of Iran and Russia decide on dividing the Caspian Sea).

This official also alluded to previous attempts to deal with the Caspian issue:

According to the 1921 and 1940 treaties, the Caspian Sea stands as the sea jointly shared by Iran and Russia and except for a ten-mile exclusive fishing zone, the rest was equally shared and exploited by the two sides. The Islamic Republic of Iran, as a country which has always pursued a policy of peaceful coexistence and relations with its neighbors, especially the Caspian Sea littoral states, has announced that a shared legal regime is the best alternative for the completion of the Caspian Sea legal system for all the littoral states.[50]

IRNA expressed further criticism of the Kaluzhny initiatives a few months later:

[Kaluzhny's remarks] on Iran's stance toward the Caspian Sea's legal status contradict the spirit of understanding and cooperation among the littoral states, especially Iran–Russian bilateral ties.[51]

An article that appeared in the Iranian journal *Resalat* was directly critical of the Kaluzhny missions on the legal status of the Caspian Sea:

Although the intention of Kaluzhny's contradictory allegations was to measure and evaluate the policies of the regional governments against Russia's viewpoint on the legal regime of the Caspian Sea, these opinions encountered different reactions from the regional countries, including Iran.

The Islamic Republic always thinks of peace and friendship in the region, and by providing the solution of Caspian Sea joint ownership, or the 20 percent share of each of the countries in this sea, it wants to maintain a state of coop-

eration and trust between the Islamic countries of the
Caspian region.

Dividing the Caspian Sea according to the naval territory
of each of the countries will destroy regional convergence
and cooperation. Moreover, the military presence of foreigners in the territory of each of these countries is far from
our expectations.

Joint ownership of the Caspian Sea obstructs the route for
foreigners to penetrate this sea, and also contributes to con-
serving its natural environment.

Kaluzhny had better not destroy the pillars of trust between
the coastal countries of the Caspian Sea, and should take
steps toward consolidating these pillars, and preventing
them from falling down.[52]

Although Iran and Russia cooperated in the Caspian
throughout most of the 1990s, united by their mutual goal of
preventing an expanded U.S. presence in the region, they
are nevertheless potential competitors as important oil producers and prospective alternative transit routes for the
region's oil and gas resources. Disagreements may emerge
over a number of issues, including pricing policies. If there
were a thaw in Washington–Tehran relations that allows Iran
to serve as a transit route for Caspian oil and gas, Iranian and
Russian interests in the region would come into conflict. In
addition, both countries are competing over the issue of gas
supply to Turkey.

Tajikistan

The case of Tajikistan further illustrates the strategic nature
of the cooperation between Iran and Russia and the importance each attaches to maintaining good relations. During
Tajikistan's civil war in the early 1990s, Tehran and Moscow
supported opposing sides. Iran gave assistance and training
to the Islamic-led insurgents who battled Russian soldiers
deployed on the border between Tajikistan and Afghanistan.

Moscow made maintaining troops on the former Soviet borders a high priority and viewed the security of the Tajik–Afghani border as especially important to its own national security. Yet despite their support for rival forces, Tehran and Moscow both recognized the importance of cooperating in the regional conflicts affecting the area. They used these conflicts as a building block for, rather than an impediment to, their bilateral relations. According to Vitaliy Naumkin:

> The existence of asymmetrical interests will not create serious problems in bilateral relations [between Iran and Russia] . . . Russia and Iran's sympathies in intra-Tajik conflict go toward different participants, but this does not impede their successful cooperation in its resolution.[53]

Russia was aware of the direct Iranian support for the Tajik rebels who were fighting Russian soldiers, as Naumkin notes:

> Moscow believed that one of the Departments of the "Kods" Headquarters—the Corps of Guards of the Islamic Revolution (CGIR), in charge of the CIS Moslem States—gave financial and advisory aid to MIRT [The Islamic Revival Party of Tajikistan], delivered arms to the Afghan–Tajik border, provided communication between the MIRT headquarters in Tehran and field commanders in the Islamic State of Afghanistan, and also trained fighters for their subsequent dispatch to Tajikistan.[54]

Following its general policy with regard to Iran in Central Asia and the Caucasus, Moscow determined that the best way to contain Tehran's support for the insurgents was to get close to Iran—especially because the leaders of the Tajik opposition had taken refuge in Iran or were under Iranian protection in Afghanistan. Russian policymakers postulated that Iranian influence over the guerrillas was better than no influence at all. At the height of the country's two disagreements over Tajikistan, Russian foreign minister Andrei Kozyrev traveled to Iran to ascertain cooperation in the conflict. Russia chose to accept Tehran as a resource for exerting influence over the rebels rather than as an antagonist. According to the Islamic Republic News Agency, "Russia [was] seeking to use Tehran's influence to persuade the opposition forces in Tajikistan to enter into negotiations with the Tajik government."[55]

In late 1993, Iran and Russia both recognized the benefits of forgoing competition for control over the negotiations and security arrangements in the region. Instead they chose to lead the processes together, in hopes of reducing the influence of Western powers, international organizations, and Pakistan. Moreover, by late 1993 the conflict had escalated to a level that alarmed Moscow and Tehran, necessitating the implementation of containment measures to prevent regional spillover.[56] In addition, it was apparent that neither country was succeeding in achieving its goals in Tajikistan. According to an article in the Iranian newspaper *Abrar*, "Russia chose Tehran as an ally so that both countries could take advantage of each other's potential capacity to fight foreign countries that were threatening their national interests."[57]

Furthermore, it seems that a shift emerged in Iran's policy toward Tajikistan in late 1993 or early 1994. Tehran halted large assistance and training to the Tajik insurgents, perhaps in part because conditions in Afghanistan made its continuance increasingly difficult. Thus, the Tajikistan episode became a turning point for Moscow and Tehran. Having achieved bilateral cooperation in controlling the conflict despite their support for rival sides, the two states thereafter experienced an accelerated improvement in their already good relations.

Afghanistan

Moscow and Tehran are on the same side of the fence (along with the United States) in supporting anti-Taliban coalitions and striving to contain the instability in Afghanistan. Moreover, Russia and Iran view the strife in Tajikistan as interlinked with the conflict in Afghanistan. As was discussed above, in late 1993 and early 1994, Russia and Iran attained a series of understandings concerning Tajikistan and Afghanistan. Their cooperation regarding Afghanistan accelerated significantly during the second half of 1998, when both sides became directly threatened by the escalation of events and the expansion of Taliban control over northern Afghanistan. In August 1998, several Iranian diplomats and reporters were kidnapped by Afghani forces and subsequently slain. Tehran threatened military action against the Taliban in response, and redeployed forces in the region.

Iran and Russia coordinate many of their policies in Afghanistan and support many joint initiatives. Apparently they cooperate, at least tacitly, on arms supplies to the United Front coalition of forces in Afghanistan. Iranian flights carrying aid to anti-Taliban fighters have landed in Tajikistan and are transported by helicopter to northern Afghanistan.[58] Russian forces control the airspace over Tajikistan and are the dominant military power there. Consequently, Iranian supply flights to factions in northern Afghanistan receive at least implicit Russian support, if not active Russian coordination. The two countries have also discussed cooperation on building a reinforced border between Iran and Afghanistan.[59]

Considering that the population of Afghanistan is almost entirely Muslim, Iran's approach to resolving the conflict there is surprising—that is, Iran emphasizes the need for representation of the various ethnic groups in the Afghani government. According to Iran's ambassador to Russia, Tehran shares Moscow's belief that "the Afghan problem cannot be settled by military means and that a government in which all political, social, and ethnic groups are represented must be formed in Afghanistan."[60]

Presumably, Russia and Iran's respective interests in the potential involvement of the various ethnic groups in Afghanistan are based on pragmatic considerations—the two states are allied with forces in Afghanistan that happen to be composed mainly of ethnic minorities. In contrast with many other regional conflicts in which Russia and Iran oppose the intrusion of international organizations (seen as providing opportunities for the United States to influence regional arrangements), the two countries support a greater UN role in

Afghanistan. The fact that the United States supports the same groups that Russia and Iran support in Afghanistan may explain their willingness to allow for a greater UN role there. Furthermore, they probably realize that the stabilization of Afghanistan will demand tremendous financial resources, which they are not in a position to provide.

Middle East

In the Middle East, Russian and Iranian interests both coincide and diverge. On the positive side, their common relations serve as an important asset for each of their standings in the region. Russia's ties with Iran (and with Iraq) keep it relevant in the Middle East; especially because of its potential arms sales, its interests and some of its wishes need to be taken into account. Iran's strategic position in the region is also enhanced through its ties to Russia, which fights against attempts to isolate Tehran.

Moscow and Tehran often serve as anchors for each other's respective involvement in the Middle East. When Russian foreign minister Igor Ivanov sought recognition for his involvement in the political efforts to quell the autumn 2000 Palestinian–Israeli confrontations, for example, he was completely sidelined by Washington, and few in the Middle East opened their doors to him. But Iranian foreign minister Kamal Kharrazi met with Ivanov in Damascus, where they issued a number of forceful joint statements and boosted the profile and prestige of the Russian diplomatic mission.

Notwithstanding the general benefits derived in the Middle East from their common relations, however, Iran and Russia's interests diverge over a number of issues in the region. For instance, their stances are completely at variance on the Arab–Israeli peace process. Iran is virulently critical of the process, opposes the very existence of the State of Israel, and actively supports groups such as Hizballah that attempt to disrupt the pursuit of peace. Russia, in contrast, is a cosponsor of the Middle East peace process and maintains warm relations with Israel. Although Iran's leaders and official media are extremely critical of the peace process, they are careful not to criticize Russia's role in it or its ties to Israel. The Iranian press does not report critically on the visits of Russian officials to Israel or vice versa. Russia does not seem willing to bend its policy toward Israel to suit Iran's desires, and the issue does not seem to cause contention between them. Moscow has even officially inquired about the safety of Jews in Iran, specifically in connection the Shiraz Jews who were tried in 2000.[61]

It is not clear whether Russia's efforts to remove the UN sanctions from Iraq and end Baghdad's international isolation have become an issue for Iran. Tehran officially supports the removal of sanctions, but it is clear that Tehran's interests are better served by Iraq's seclusion and debilitation. In actuality, it is probably pleased that the sanctions are still in place.

In the early 1990s, Russia's attempts to develop close ties with Iran's previous rivals in the Persian Gulf and its efforts to sell them arms created disagreements between Moscow and Tehran. Changes within Iran have led to the lessening of its tensions with the Gulf states and facilitated its participation in forums with them, decreasing the saliency of this issue.

The Balkans

Russia and Iran's responses to each other's positions on the Balkan conflicts of the 1990s illustrate the strength of their bilateral relations. The two states supported rival forces in most of those conflicts. As with Central Asia and the Caucasus, however, Russia and Iran were united in their opposition to an expanded U.S. influence in the region, and they often cooperated to undermine U.S. efforts. They took similar stands in the United Nations and other international bodies in criticizing U.S. actions in the Balkans, despite their support for rival groups. In a few instances, Iran published harsh criticisms of Moscow's actions in the area, but those outbursts did not affect their collaboration in peacekeeping and other international forums.[62]

In the second half of the 1990s, once Russia and Iran's relations had developed into wider cooperation, their diverging positions in various regional conflicts did not have a significant impact on their bilateral ties. That development attests to the strength and importance they both attach to those ties.

Economic Cooperation and Trade

Since the Soviet breakup, trade between Russia and Iran has been quite modest. Tehran's debts and failures to meet its financial commitments to Russia have been a source of disagreement between the two countries and have slowed their cooperation in a number of fields. Tehran's problems paying Russia served as the chief restraint on arms sales and created lags in the provision of civil nuclear power plants and the delivery schedule of the Kilo submarines to Iran. It also led to the cancellation of planned uranium shipments to Iran in 1995. At a number of junctures, however, they have succeeded in renegotiating payment arrangements and overcoming obstacles, and the issue has not had a significantly adverse effect on their overall relations. These developments are especially interesting, considering that important economic actors in Russia have placed great hopes on the financial benefits that could accrue from relations with Iran.[63] Iran's trade with some of the other Soviet successor states managed to recover from the sharp decline that ensued after the Soviet collapse. But trade with Russia has remained relatively small. From 1993 to 1996, it declined from $723 million to $200 million. In 1997 it rose to $450 million.[64] The volume of trade between the two countries continued to increase slightly in 1998 to $546 million, and in 1999 it remained at approximately the same level.[65]

According to the Iranian newspaper *Abrar*, the Soviet Union prior to its disintegration ranked variously as Iran's first- to third-largest partner for non-oil exports, and second- to fifth-largest partner for imports. In the mid-1990s, Russia ranked eighteenth for imports and twentieth for exports among Iran's trade partners.[66] The modest trade flow that currently exists between the two countries works in Russia's favor, as its exports to Iran are significantly greater than its imports. A report released by Iranian customs in 1996 indicated that "[Iranian] imports from Russia were six times Iran's exports to that country."[67] Press sources reported that Iran's debt to Russia in 1995 stood at $582 million, of which $380 million was owed to the former state arms company Rosvooruzhenie and $170 million to the trade firm Tekhnopromexport.[68]

Politicians and commentators in both states have frequently discussed the financial disputes between the countries.[69] In 1992, when Iran suspended payments on its military debt to Russia, and in return Russia suspended payments on its foreign debt, Russian minister for foreign economic relations Oleg Davidov openly stated:

> Russo–Iranian trade has decreased at a rather rapid pace due to Iran's lack of finances. Therefore, the construction of facilities in Iranian territory—electric heating and power plants and nuclear power stations—is proceeding with great difficulty. Iran repays very little and, at times, we lack funds even for the maintenance of our specialists. This also applies to the delivery of special equipment.[70]

The two countries have attempted to improve and institutionalize the trade between them through the establishment of the Permanent Russian–Iranian Intergovernmental Commission for Economic Cooperation, headed in December 1996 by the vice-premier of the Russian government and the minister of the economy and finances in Iran. Some of the cooperation between the two countries, especially economic cooperation, has been conducted directly on the province-to-province level, with both Moscow and Tehran's encouragement.[71] The Russian provinces of Astrakhan, Tatarstan, Kalmykia, and Komi and the Iranian regions of Gilan and Mazandaran are especially active in these pursuits. At the same time, the three Iranian provinces inhabited primarily by ethnic Azerbaijanis conduct significant bilateral trade with Azerbaijan, and the Khorasan province, with its large Turkmen population, trades with Turkmenistan. Russia and Iran have encouraged their provinces to engage in direct cooperation and trade, creating a mechanism that is sometimes useful for circumventing bureaucratic obstacles and detaching trade issues from other international concerns.

In its efforts to expand trade ties with Tehran, Russia has expressed an interest in joining or being associated with the Economic Cooperation Organization (ECO), an organization that Iran leads. Members of this group include the states of Central Asia, Azerbaijan, Pakistan, Afghanistan, and Turkey. Despite its frequent and highly publicized summits, the ECO has not been able to generate cooperation that extends beyond the existing trade ties of its member countries.

Two different trends might affect trade between Russia and Iran in the near future. In one scenario, high oil prices would enable Iran to pay for more goods from Russia, including military hardware, thus providing opportunities for increased trade. The first indications that oil prices were on the rise may have influenced Moscow's decision in late 1999 to openly declare its interest in concluding new arms deals with Iran, on the assumption that actual payment potential had increased. In addition to the rise in its oil income, Iran's debt is significantly lower and foreign investment in its oil industry is beginning to show promise, offering the prospect of even higher oil income in the coming year. At the same time, however, the second trend that could affect cooperation between Russia and Iran is the possible rapprochement between Washington and Tehran. The relaxation of U.S. sanctions on Iran has convinced some important members of the business community within the Islamic Republic that a renewal of trade with the United States is imminent. Consequently, they are delaying any new trade deals with Russia in order to improve their chances for renewed trade ties with the United States.

Notes

1. Islamic Republic News Agency (IRNA), March 7, 1996.
2. Itar-Tass in English, April 8, 1995.
3. This domestic political interest has continued to be relevant under President Vladimir Putin.

4. Vitaliy Naumkin, "The Russian–Iranian Relations: Present Status and Prospects for the Future," *Perceptions* (March–May 1998), p. 67.

5. IRNA in English, November 29, 1999.

6. Naumkin, p. 67.

7. Ibid., p. 77.

8. *Abrar*, July 4, 1995 (FBIS-NES-95-134).

9. IRNA in English, January 6, 1995.

10. Interfax in English, January 14, 2000; Reuters, January 15, 2000.

11. Interfax in English, September 27, 1999.

12. *Izvestiia*, quoted in *Iran Times*, September 1, 2000.

13. Itar-Tass, December 27, 2000.

14. Naumkin, p. 80.

15. See *Segodnia*, May 26, 1995, p. 9.

16. Viktor Vishniakov, "Russian–Iranian Relations and Regional Stability," *International Affairs* 45, no. 1, p. 151.

17. Interview with Ambassador Tretyakov, *Abrar*, August 10, 1993 (FBIS-NES93-163).

18. Alexei G. Arbatov, "Russian Foreign Policy Priorities for the 1990s," in *Russian Security After the Cold War: Seven Views from Moscow* (Washington: Brassey's, 1994), p. 11.

19. Voice of the Islamic Republic of Iran in English, January 12, 2000.

20. *Tehran Times*, December 30, 1991, p. 2.

21. For a comparative look at the use of Islam instrumentally to support regime goals, see Jessica Stern, "Pakistan's Jihad Culture," *Foreign Affairs* (November/December 2000).

22. Arbatov, pp. 26–27.

23. IRNA in English, June 28, 1995.

24. Vishniakov, p. 152.

25. Interfax, December 19, 1997.

26. IRNA in English, October 24, 1995.

27. Tehran Voice of the Islamic Republic of Iran, November 28, 1999.

28. IRNA in English, November 29, 1999.

29. Interfax in English, November 28, 1999.

30. *Jomhuri-ye Islami*, November 14, 1999, pp. 1, 2, 14 (FBIS-NES-1999-1221); See also, *Jomhuri-ye Islami*, November 25, 1999, p. 2 (FBIS-NES-2000-0114); *Jomhuri-ye Islami*, December 8, 1999, pp. 1, 2 (FBIS-NES-2000-0113).

31. For instance, *Kayhan International* in English, December 21, 1999, p. 2 (FBIS-NES-2000-0107).

32. *Jomhuri-ye Islami*, October 9, 1999, p. 12 (FBIS-NES-1999-1201) (emphasis added).

33. Voice of the Islamic Republic of Iran, January 6, 1995 (FBIS-NES-95-005).

34. Voice of the Islamic Republic of Iran, January 12, 1995 (FBIS-NES-95-008).

35. *Ettela'at*, April 3, 1995, p. 2 (FBIS-NES-95-075).

36. See statement of the Russian minister of atomic energy, quoted IRNA in English, January 6, 1995 (FBIS-NES-95-005), following very mild Iranian official reaction to the first Chechen conflict, Voice of Islamic Republic of Iran, January 4, 1995 (FBIS-NES-95-003).

37. Itar-Tass, September 24, 1999.

38. The statement refers to the incursion of Chechen combatants into the neighboring autonomous Russian republic of Dagestan in August 1999, which served as the pretext for Moscow's onslaught on Chechnya.

39. Interfax in English, September 28, 1999.

40. *Kayhan International* in English, November 28, 1999, p. 4 (FBIS-NES-1999-1206).

41. *Iran News* (Internet version), December 6, 1999.

42. IRNA in English, November 28, 1999.

43. *Asr-e Ma* (Tehran), January 19, 2000, p. 8.

44. Since early 2001, Moscow has reduced much of its open opposition to Baku–Ceyhan. They want the bulk of the resources to flow on north-south routes through their territories.

45. See Lucian Pugliaresi, "Energy Security: How Valuable is Caspian Oil?" *Caspian Studies Program Policy Brief*, no. 3 (Cambridge: Harvard University, 2001).

46. The fact that the sides often invoke these treaties as justification for their stances on the Caspian status is quite intriguing considering that Iran has repeatedly declared these treaties as invalid and nonbinding and in light of the fact that during the Soviet period, both sides explored the energy resources in the sea on a separate basis, setting the border between them in the middle of the sea.

47. For instance, when Azerbaijani president Heydar Aliyev announced his willingness to allow Iranian participation (5 percent) in the consortium developing Caspian oil in November 1994, Iran was willing to abandon its legal stance.

48. See, for instance *Abrar*, July 4, 1995 (FBIS-NES-95-134).

49. *Resalat*, February 15, 1998, p. 16.

50. IRNA, September 25, 2000.

51. IRNA, November 12, 2000.

52. *Resalat*, August 1, 2000, p. 13.

53. Naumkin, p. 70.

54. Ibid, p. 73.

55. Interfax in English, March 31, 1993. Also see IRNA in English, November 6, 1993.

56. Voice of the Islamic Republic of Iran, September 15, 1993 (FBIS-NES-93-177).

57. *Abrar*, July 17, 1994, p. 12 (FBIS-NES-94-143).

58. Lecture by Julie Siers, Washington D.C., April 2000.

59. Itar-Tass, November 29, 2000.

60. Interfax in English, February 16, 2000.

61. Itar-Tass in English, June 11, 1999.

62. For an example of this type of criticism, see *Tehran Times*, December 4, 1994, p. 2.

63. For an in-depth analysis of the interests of certain Russian economic sectors in relations with Iran, see Eugene Rumer, *Dangerous Drift: Russia's Middle East Policy*, Policy Papers no. 54 (Washington, D.C.: The Washington Institute for Near East Policy, 2000).

64. Naumkin, p. 78.

65. IRNA in English, January 11, 2000.

66. *Abrar*, June 10, 1996, p. 4 (FBIS-NES-96-116).

67. Ibid.

68. Interfax in English, September 19, 1996.

69. For instance, IRNA in English, August 4, 1992; IRNA in English May 31, 1995; Interfax in English, January 4, 1996.

70. Itar-Tass in English, May 5, 1995 (FBIS-SOV-95-088).

71. IRNA, June 22, 1999; IRNA in English, February 2, 2000.

Chapter 4

Arms and Strategic Weapons
Cooperation

"Our trump card is broad cooperation in the sphere of
nuclear technologies, which in time will help our partners reduce their dependence on Russia. This is very
important to any country. Although, of course, it is also a
good carrot—however you want to describe it. We will get
into the market today, one way or another."
— *Viktor Mikhailov, director of MINATOM, quoted in*
Priroda, *August 1995*

In the past decade, Iran has made significant progress in its
attempts to acquire weapons of mass destruction (WMD)
and ballistic missile technologies. According to U.S. government reports and the testimony of U.S. senior officials, Russian
companies and government ministries have played important
roles in the advancement of these capabilities. Russian entities, with or without the support of the central government,
have provided a range of technologies crucial to the progress
of Iran's long-range missile programs and have reportedly
assisted in both chemical and biological warfare development
as well.[1] In addition, during the 1990s, Russia sold to Iran
conventional arms that included tanks, combat aircraft, and
diesel-powered submarines. Russia also agreed to build light-
water nuclear reactors in Bushehr, and construction of these
facilities is already underway. Although these light-water reactors are a civil nuclear project and do not directly contribute
to the advancement of Iran's nuclear capability, the overall
framework of this project may have provided an opportunity
for Iran to acquire additional technologies, equipment, and
materials. Moreover, representatives of Russia's Ministry of
Atomic Energy had agreed to provide Iran with a gas centri-

fuge and laser technologies for uranium enrichment, but both offers were cancelled at Washington's request. Shipments of graphite and heavy-water technologies related to plutonium production were also cancelled.

Several factors explain Russia's assistance to Iran's energy and weapons programs. In the overall framework of Russian–Iranian relations, the two states see each other as strategic partners who together are able to counterbalance a unipolar U.S.-dominated world. Furthermore, Russia and Iran share a number of top-level strategic priorities, and Russia does not view Iran as a likely threat. It needs Iranian cooperation in order to contend with immediate challenges to its security, such as the situation in Chechnya, and it will not risk that cooperation to avert possible long-term, indefinite threats. Moreover, one should consider Russia's perception of the potential threats Iran poses in Central Asia and the Caucasus in order to understand its attitude toward Iranian WMD. Russia believes that through cooperation and frequent contacts, it will be able to maintain more leverage over Iran's actions. Even as it sees Iran as a strategic partner, however, Russia also strives for cooperative and sound relations with the United States. Most Russian policymakers do not want Iran to develop WMD.

There are three possible explanations for Russia's cooperation with Iran in the advancement of Tehran's programs for WMD. The first explanation suggests that the Russian government is doing its best to control the flow of technology and materials to Iran but is not successfully controlling various organizations, ministries, and other concerns within Russia. According to a second possible explanation, Russia is striving to maintain an especially cooperative relationship with Iran and is willing to acquiesce to many of Tehran's requests in military fields to foster it. In this scenario, Moscow is doing little to obstruct the outflow of materials, technology, and equipment—even as it publicly accedes to U.S. demands, in order to maintain good relations with Washington. A third possible explanation is that Russia is attempting to "muddle through" by meeting some of Iran's requests and promoting a cooperative relationship, while refusing to provide the kind of technology, materials, and equipment that bear directly on Iran's WMD capability (and which the United States finds particularly objectionable).

The Russian contribution to Iran's advancement of its WMD programs most likely derives from a combination of these models, and the pattern of cooperation has changed throughout the decade. Furthermore, Russia cooperates differently with Iran in the three separate spheres of missile production, conventional arms, and nuclear capability. In some fields, especially missile production, individual Russian companies and government agencies have apparently cooperated with Iranian institutions on their own initiative rather than through central, officially sanctioned channels. At times, Moscow has been quite lax in regulating these groups' activities. Regarding conventional weapons, it is not clear if Russia's commitment to the United States to refrain from new arms sales to Iran was made in good faith, as Moscow has done little to limit arms shipments. In the nuclear sphere, Russia views Iran as a friendly country and is willing to risk that its activities will help advance Iran's nuclear program in order to preserve the overall framework of their relations. But the United States has been successful in getting Russia to abstain from activities that directly contribute to the acceleration and advancement of Iran's nuclear weapons program.

Russian–Iranian cooperation in arms sales and nuclear energy is intertwined with other aspects of their relations. Russian officials have stated that military-technical cooperation is an important aspect of their bilateral relations. In the words of Viktor Vishniakov:

> A broader cooperation between Russia and Iran in the military sphere would make it possible to end the suspicion lingering from old times and help resolve the issue of Russian border guards on Armenia and Turkmenistan's borders with Iran; [to] more efficiently fulfill contracts on the delivery to Iran and subsequent servicing and maintenance

of Russian weapons and combat equipment; [and to] create an atmosphere of confidence and make for a more balanced assessment of the military and strategic situation in
the region.[2]

Throughout the past decade, Russia's cooperation with
Iran on arms sales and in the advancement of its ability to
acquire WMD has been a central item on the agenda of U.S.–
Russian relations. During the Clinton administration, Russia
made a number of commitments to the United States to abstain from new conventional arms sales as well as cooperation
in fields that could contribute to the advancement of Iran's
WMD program. Those commitments included refraining
from activities considered legal under the international regimes that regulate this field—even the Nuclear Suppliers
Group guidelines.

The interpretation of these commitments was a source of
frequent contention between Moscow and Washington
throughout the Clinton era. One of the major issues of dis-
pute has been the determination of what Russia's commitment
not to engage in cooperation that could advance Iran's acquisition of nuclear weapons actually entails. Washington
maintains that Iran has taken advantage of the framework of
civil nuclear cooperation with Russia to acquire the technology, materials, and equipment that have advanced its nuclear
capability. Moscow contends that Iran, as a signatory in good
standing to the Nuclear Nonproliferation Treaty (NPT), is
entitled to assistance in the domain of civil nuclear energy
and that cooperation between the two countries conforms to
the treaty. In addition, Russia and the United States are divided in their interpretation of Moscow's compliance with its
promise not to engage in additional civil nuclear cooperation with Iran "beyond the Bushehr project." The United
States understands this commitment (under the Gore–
Chernomyrdin Agreement) to mean no more provisions
beyond one light-water reactor, while Russia asserts that it can
supply a number of reactors at Bushehr and can share additional technologies and equipment.

The framework of Russian commitments to the United States regarding military cooperation with Iran broke down on the eve of the November 2000 U.S. presidential election, when Russia canceled its commitment to not make any new conventional arms deals with Iran after 1999. This renunciation was followed by Defense Minister Igor Sergeyev's visit to Tehran in December 2000. Iranian acquisition capabilities— which have been galvanized by rising oil prices, coupled with Russia's assertion of a foreign policy that is independent of Washington's wishes—will land Russian–Iranian strategic cooperation on the agenda of the major foreign policy challenges for the Bush administration.

Russia's Contributions to Iranian WMD and Strategic Weapons Programs

According to official reports, the testimonies of senior U.S. officials responsible for nonproliferation, and a number of independent researchers, Iran is pursuing the development of ballistic missile delivery systems, as well as WMD in the nuclear, chemical, and biological spheres.[3] In his testimony before the Senate, Assistant Secretary of State for Nonproliferation Robert Einhorn declared:

> Iran is seeking aggressively to acquire equipment, materiel, and technology from abroad in an effort to establish the capability to produce nonconventional weapons indigenously and thereby to insulate those weapons programs from outside pressures.[4]

Among all the fields in which it is attempting to acquire WMD, Iran has made the most progress in the field of ballistic missiles. Russian companies and ministries, sometimes with government approval and sometimes illicitly, have played an important role in Iran's advances.

Nuclear Technology and Weapons

According to U.S. officials, evidence that Tehran is attempting to acquire the means to produce highly enriched uranium and plutonium provide some of the most convincing signs that Iran is pursuing a nuclear weapons program.[5] Assistant Secretary of State for Nonproliferation Robert Einhorn said in testimony before the Senate Foreign Relations Committee, "Neither of these capabilities is necessary to meet Iran's declared desire to have a civil nuclear power program to generate electricity, which is itself suspicious in light of Iran's abundant oil resources." He also explained that organizations subordinate to the Russian Ministry for Atomic Energy (MINATOM) have contributed to the advancement of the Iranian nuclear program:

> Russia remains the one significant exception to the virtual embargo on nuclear cooperation with Iran. The most visible nuclear cooperation between the two countries is Russia's construction of a 1000-megawatt nuclear power reactor at Bushehr, Iran. We have opposed this project, not because we believe such a light-water reactor under International Atomic Energy Agency safeguards itself poses a serious proliferation threat, but because of our concern that the Bushehr project would be used by Iran as a cover for maintaining wide-ranging contacts with Russia's nuclear entities and for engaging in more sensitive forms of cooperation with more direct applicability to a nuclear weapons program. While refusing to halt the power reactor sale, the Russians have argued that they are just as opposed as we are to an Iranian nuclear weapons capability. We are aware that Russian entities—most of them subordinate to MINATOM, the Russian Ministry of Atomic Energy—have engaged in extensive cooperation with Iranian nuclear research centers that are outside the bounds of the Bushehr project. Much of this assistance involves technologies with direct application to the production of weapons-grade fissile materials, including research reactors, heavy-water production technology, and laser-isotope separation technology for enriching uranium.[6]

The main U.S. concern regarding the Bushehr project center is that Russia, in order to both entice Iran to continue to buy these civil nuclear reactors and to reciprocate Iranian goodwill in other areas of their mutual interest, may overtly or covertly be committing to sell other technologies to Iran. Among the suspected technologies are components of graphite reactors and heavy-water reactors, both suitable for plutonium production, and the laser technology used for extremely small-scale production of HEU (Highly Enriched Uranium). Moreover, Bushehr provides a framework for training Iranian nuclear scientists in Russia, and it allows Iran to develop additional contracts and cooperation with Russian nuclear institutes that may lead to sanctioned or unsanctioned provision of other sensitive nuclear technology. In addition, the Bushehr project increases Iran's overall base of nuclear knowledge and expertise.

Russia's first commitment to cooperate with Iran in the civil nuclear sphere was when the two countries signed an agreement during Majlis Speaker Akbar Hashemi Rafsanjani's visit to Moscow in 1989, prior to the Soviet breakup.[7] This protocol was expanded in the summer of 1992, when two intergovernmental agreements were signed: the first on cooperation in the development of nuclear energy for peaceful purposes, the second on the construction of an atomic power plant in Bushehr.[8] Viktor Mikhailov, then the director of MINATOM, indicated that the first agreement:

> [E]nvisaged in its sections basic and applied research, preparation and training of specialists, research in the problem of nuclear power plant security, [the sharing of] experience accumulated in the operation of these plants, the development of support systems and radiological protection systems, and the production and application of radioisotopes . . . Thus, you can see that this is a fairly broad program overall.[9]

In 1993, an additional agreement was signed between Russia and Iran that specified the terms of supply for the atomic power plant in Bushehr. Conditions and timetables have been renegotiated a number of times since. In 1995, the United States discovered that the Bushehr deal encompassed an extensive plan for supplying materials and training Iranian specialists. The most significant discovery concerned the Russian agreement to supply a gas centrifuge plant, which can be used for uranium enrichment. According to the agreement signed between Mikhailov and Reza Amrollahi, who served as Iran's vice president and chairman of its Atomic Energy Organization, stipulated that

> The parties will instruct their competent organizations to prepare and sign: in three months a contract for delivery of a light-water reactor for research with a power of 30-50 Megawatt Thermal (MWt) from Russia; in the first quarter of 1995, a contract for the delivery of 2,000 tons of natural uranium from Russia; in the first quarter of 1995, a contract for the preparation/training for Atomic Energy Organization of Iran scientific personnel, 10–20 (graduate students and Ph.D.s) annually at Russian institutions; within six months' time, a contract for the construction of a uranium mine in Iran, after which negotiations will be conducted for the signing of a contract for the construction of a centrifuge plant for enrichment of uranium according to conditions, which are comparable to conditions of contracts concluded by Russian organizations with firms in other countries.[10]

The centrifuge plant could have significantly contributed to Iran's ability to produce nuclear weapons. Following the U.S. discovery of this Russian–Iranian agreement, President Boris Yeltsin announced:

> The point is that the contract was concluded legitimately and in accordance with international law, and no international treaties were violated in the process. But it is true that the contract does contain components of peaceful and military nuclear energy. Now we have agreed to separate those two.
>
> Inasmuch as they relate to . . . the potential for creating weapons-grade fuel and other matters, the centrifuge, the

construction of silos, and so on—we have decided to exclude those aspects from the contract, so the military component falls away, and what remains is just a peaceful nuclear power station on light-water reactors, which is designed to provide heat and energy.[11]

In effect, Yeltsin canceled the proposed sale of the centrifuge and other aspects of the cooperation. Even after the U.S. discovery of the centrifuge deal, Mikhailov claimed that the centrifuge had only been discussed as a possibility in talks with the Iranians, and that no actual contract had been signed for its supply.

Moscow is currently working to finish the construction of a light-water nuclear reactor (VVER-1000) at the Bushehr complex. Deputy Atomic Energy Minister Yevgenii Reshetnikov announced on February 21, 2001, that the construction of the reactor should be completed by the end of 2003.[12] In addition, the two sides have agreed in principle to the supply and construction of three additional reactors (an additional VVER-1000 and two VVER-400s at Bushehr). The value of the contract for the first reactor is estimated at $780 million to $1 billion, and the price of the three additional reactors will reach a total of approximately $3 billion.

The Bushehr project has encountered many scheduling problems, and its timetable for completion has been revised several times. According to official Russian announcements, the delays were usually caused by Iran's difficulties in paying for the project. Some work stoppages occurred because of discrepancies regarding the design of the reactor and questions about whether Russian or Iranian contractors would construct particular aspects of the facility. Difficulties have also emerged in attempting to apply Russian technology to the German-designed reactors. In 1998, the partners indicated that Russia would supply Iran with a turnkey reactor built mostly by Russian contractors. In January 2001, Russia announced it had begun construction of a second reactor at Bushehr.

Despite constant and considerable pressure from Washington—including executive and congressional sanctions, penalties on Russian companies that have engaged in this cooperation with Iran, and cancellation of contracts for projects with Russia—Moscow has refused to renounce the Bushehr project. In 1995 it promised the United States not to provide any nuclear facilities to Iran "beyond Bushehr." The United States interpreted that promise to mean only one reactor; apparently Russia believes it is within its rights to provide up to four reactors to Iran.

Mikhailov observed in *Priroda* that Moscow's trump card in attracting customers to Russian civil nuclear projects is its willingness to provide materials and technology that Western contractors are not willing to supply:

> There is no way Russia can entice customers today while the West and the Americans are providing credits, as is happening in China. Our trump card is broad cooperation in the sphere of nuclear technologies, which in time will help our partners reduce their dependence on Russia. This is very important to any country. Although, of course, it is also a good carrot—however you want to describe it. We will get into the market today one way or another.[13]

It is precisely these technologies and materials that are useful for advancing nuclear weapons programs. Since the canceling of the centrifuge deal, however, there is no evidence that Russia's current policy includes the provision of an independent fuel-cycle capability to Iran. Mikhailov has unequivocally stated that Iran had persistently asked about the centrifuges:

> Naturally, when we get together—and this happens once a year—we go over all the articles of the agreement. We say, here you need to send specialists for training, you have to look at these aspects of the fuel cycle . . . And when they propose that we discuss the question of centrifuges, we reply that they first need a mine and an ore-processing plant. After that, we can discuss centrifuges. Everything is entered into the negotiations protocol. Of course, if you really wanted to see it a certain way, this could be presented as almost a military transaction, and they could pretend to have stopped it. Naturally, there is nothing of this kind here.[14]

Mikhailov has held this deal before the Iranian government as a carrot, to entice Tehran to pay for civil nuclear reactors. In response to an interviewer's question as to whether he is dangling the supply of a centrifuge as a potential incentive for Iran, he said:

> You could put it that way. Of course, if we build a centrifuge plant for them today, it will stand idle, even if they have military plans in mind. It will simply stand idle. They have nothing right now, just their own natural uranium. The ore must be extracted and processed, then natural uranium obtained. Only then can they engage in enrichment.[15]

Many Russian officials and some Western analysts have attempted to dismiss the centrifuge deal as a personal initiative conducted by Mikhailov and MINATOM, rather than an officially sanctioned policy of the Russian government. But if that were so, Mikhailov would have been dismissed from his position as head of MINATOM with the discovery of the centrifuge agreement in 1995. Instead, he remained in that position until 1998. Moreover, his successor, Yevgenii Adamov, has been even more aggressively involved in cooperation with Iran; his involvement in the laser and graphite reactor deals predated his appointment as minister. Indeed, the very fact of Adamov's appointment, considering his intense involvement in advancing nuclear cooperation with Iran, testifies to the Russian government's implicit approval of these activities.

As was pointed out by Mikhailov, the agreements with Iran included quite "broad cooperation," including the training of Iranian specialists. In addition, representatives of Iran's nuclear energy complex and missile programs have direct contacts with Russian scientific institutes and universities, including the State University of Moscow and the Institute of Nuclear Research in Dubna.[16] These ties provide opportunities to acquire knowledge and materials that could advance Iranian WMD programs. As he had done with the centrifuges, Mikhailov offered the prospect of flexibility on the fuel arrangements as an inducement:

> I cannot grant them credits today. I can only promise that if
> cooperation develops and nuclear power plants are built,
> we are prepared to examine on a broader scale all aspects
> of fuel production for these power plants.[17]

MINATOM was the driving force behind Russian sales of
civil nuclear energy plants.[18] This drive extends far beyond
the self-serving profit desires of this organization and its members. MINATOM's current chief, Adamov, holds a vision of
Russia's future in which civil nuclear energy exports play a
key role. He envisions Russia as the leader in the development of new technologies that will turn civil nuclear power
into a safe and "green" energy source, solving many of the
world's energy and environmental problems. Through this
leadership, in Adamov's estimation, Russia will emerge from
its economic bleakness to become a great power once again.[19]

Representatives of MINATOM have asserted that by selling items and technology not generally included in U.S. civil
nuclear plant sales, Russia can gain a competitive edge. Client states, however, can also utilize these nuclear technologies
to advance their WMD programs.

As has been discussed above, Moscow often rewarded
Tehran for its support in Chechnya with promises to provide
Iran with much sought-after nuclear reactors, and Iranian
security delegations continued to visit Moscow during the war
with the Chechens.[20] Moreover, Russia believes that uphold-
ing its commitments to sell arms and nuclear power plants is
essential to preserving its credibility and prestige in Tehran's
eyes—to remaining, in the perception of its neighbors, an
important power to be reckoned with. In Moscow's view, concessions to the United States on these types of issues might
encourage Iran to seek other associations.[21] Moscow's agreement to supply nuclear reactors to Tehran has become the
litmus test of their bilateral relationship. According to the
Iranian daily *Abrar,* Russia's ambassador to Iran observed, "The
developments in Russian–Iranian nuclear cooperation
showed that Moscow is not willing, in any way, to sacrifice its
relations with Iran."[22]

Russian representatives claim that as long as Iran is attempting to develop a nuclear weapons program, it is

preferable for Moscow to control this program and intelligence information. In this context, Mikhailov compared Russia's relationship with Iran to its nuclear cooperation with China and stated:

> We, in addition to the IAEA [International Atomic Energy Agency], control production in Iran as in the case with China, for example. Our team must be located at the facility, preventing anything from being concealed. Even if Iran withdraws from the IAEA, Russian control remains. If Russian control of the facility is threatened, we simply dismantle it and take out all the equipment.[23]

The United States' demands that Russia refrain from selling weapons and technology to Iran are, according to Moscow, a competitor's attempt to push Russia out of the world arms and energy markets. Many Russian policymakers believe that renewed U.S.-Iranian relations are imminent; accordingly, they contend, the United States wants to preserve the Iranian market for its own sales.[24] Adamov voiced his support for Russia's supplying Iran with additional nuclear reactors and expanded cooperation before the United States is in a position to do so: "We don't want to lose ten or even fifteen years, during which the United States will gradually improve its relations with Iran."[25] Russia believes that if Moscow doesn't sell to Iran, someone else will. Russians often name China, France, and eventually the United States as potential suppliers of nuclear power plants to Iran.

Some Russian commentators have suggested that the U.S. desire to halt the sale of Russian nuclear technologies to Iran stems from a part of a larger campaign to preserve American interests on the expanding world market for nuclear power plants:

> What is behind such threats may be not only U.S. concern over the problem of international terrorism, but the desire to gain unchallenged leadership on the rapidly expanding world market for nuclear power plants.
>
> Those who have achieved leading positions on this market now will get a powerful source of earnings in the future, to

say nothing of certain political influence in the customer countries, because the trade in nuclear power plants remains a politicized business sector. For this reason, the trade war on the nuclear power plant market that the United States unleashed against Russia in late 1994 is unprecedented—in terms of the fierceness of the struggle (up to and including the threat of deterioration of bilateral political relations) and the value of victory: the victor will gain potential access to immense money that cannot be earned even in the small arms trade, which is the most profitable business today.[26]

Yet despite this feeling of inevitability, most Russian policymakers do not want Iran to become a nuclear power or to advance its WMD programs. But, especially in off-the-record situations, some Russian strategists and commentators have suggested that, given Russia's clear strategic inferiority to the United States and Washington's perceived intransigence on comprehensive disarmament, Moscow stands to gain from the emergence of multiple nuclear powers. They believe that such a development, despite the inherent risks involved, would complicate U.S. calculations regarding Russia in the nuclear sphere, and offset some of Russia's inferiority.

Ballistic Missile Program

Iran is actively developing an ambitious ballistic missile program. According to U.S. government reports and testimony, Iran has already deployed hundreds of SCUD missiles and can produce them domestically. It has conducted three tests of the Shahab-3 missile—one in 1998, two in 2000. This medium-range ballistic missile, which has a reach of 1,200 kilometers, can hit Turkey, Saudi Arabia, and Israel, as well as U.S. forces in the Persian Gulf. Iran has publicly displayed three Shahab-3s, along with a mobile launcher and other ground-support equipment. According to statements by government officials, Iran is developing long-range missiles as well; the defense minister has announced the country's intention of developing Shahab-4 and Shahab-5 programs.[27]

Russia and North Korea have provided extensive assistance to Iran's ballistic missile program. Russian technology gave a significant boost to the Shahab-3 program, cutting years from its expected development period.[28] In February 2001, U.S. Central Intelligence Agency chief George Tenet commented that Iran continues to receive Russian missile technology and "has one of the largest and most capable ballistic missile programs in the Middle East."[29] Russian aerospace organizations and individual scientists reportedly contributed to the conversion of an improved version of the North Korean No Dong missile into the Shahab-3.[30] Among the Russian institutions and companies that have played a prominent role in assistance to Iran's ballistic missile program are the Moscow Aviation Institute, the Baltic State Technical University, and the Scientific Research and Design Institute of Power Technology (NIKIET).

In response to Russia's activities, the United States levied sanctions on a number of Russian institutions, including the government-owned space-technology marketing agency Glavkosmos, the aerospace materials research institute NIIGrafit, the guidance technology developer Polyus, and several smaller and less prominent entities. Furthermore, the United States has imposed restrictions on two major Russian educational entities, the Moscow Aviation Institute and the Baltic State Technical University.

Despite the U.S. sanctions on Russian entities that have assisted Iran in missile development, Russia persists in its commitment to cooperate with Iran in this sphere. During his December 2000 visit to Iran, Sergeyev toured plants connected with the Iranian missile production program.[31] According to the Islamic Republic News Agency (IRNA), he devoted his "main attention to the technology of production of portable and stationary short-range missiles, including anti-tank [missiles], as well as air-to-surface missiles." According to Itar-Tass, Sergeyev visited Iran's aerospace organization in order to familiarize himself with Iran's "rocket production problems" and weapons specifications.[32]

Chemical and Biological Weapons

Iran began its chemical weapons (CW) program during the Iran–Iraq war in response to Iraq's use of chemical weapons.

Despite Iran's 1997 ratification of the Chemical Weapons Convention (CWC), U.S. officials believe that Iran has maintained a CW program and a substantial stockpile of weaponized and bulk agent. [33] In his testimony to the Senate Committee on Foreign Relations, John Lauder, director of the Directorate of Central Intelligence's Nonproliferation Center, explained:

> Tehran's goals for its CW program for the past decade have been to expand its production capability and stockpile, [to] reach self-sufficiency by acquiring the means to manufacture chemical production equipment and precursors, and [to] diversify its CW arsenal by producing more sophisticated and lethal agents and munitions.[34]

Lauder also testified that during 1999 "Russian entities provided production technology, training, and expertise that Iran could use to create a more advanced and self-sufficient CW infrastructure."[35]

U.S. officials believe that Iran also possesses biological weapons, mostly in the research and development stage. Iranian entities have sought materials for this program and expertise from foreign suppliers in both Russia and Western Europe.

Conventional Arms Sales

A number of existing conditions, listed below, make Iran and Russia more likely to engage in intensive arms sales:

- Strapped for cash, Russia is in ardent search of arms sales markets.
- U.S. sanctions on Iran limit that country's potential suppliers for weapons and technology.
- Russia is interested in retaining a position of influence in the Middle East, and arms sales can help it achieve this goal.[36]
- Many high-level Russian policymakers and members of military-industrial circles have extensive connections in

Iran and a positive inclination toward the state.
- Iran currently faces multiple security threats.

But many additional factors combined to limit Russia's arms sales to Iran in the 1990s to modest amounts:

- Tehran wants to be able to produce its own major weapons systems rather than acquiring completed arms.
- The chief aim of Russian weapons sales today is economic, and Iran has had a poor payment record and limited means for hard-currency payment.
- Russian weapons systems have a relatively poor reputation among the Iranian military. There is still no consensus in Iran to convert what are predominantly Western weapons systems to Russian ones.
- The Russian commitment to the United States not to sign new arms deals with Iran has limited Russia and Iran's ability to conclude major sales. Thus, between 1994 and 1997, Russian arms transfers to Iran were valued at only about $700 million.[37]

Notably, Russia apparently does not perceive a threat from the potential buildup of Iran's conventional forces. Nor does it fear that arms it supplies to Tehran will end up in conflict zones where Russia is involved.

U.S.–Russian cooperation on Iranian proliferation began in 1994, when Yeltsin pledged to President Bill Clinton that Russia would not conclude any new arms contracts with Iran, would honor only its existing agreements, and would complete the arms transfers within those agreements by the end of 1999. In return, Washington promised not to sanction the Russian companies fulfilling established contracts to Iran. That agreement between Yeltsin and Clinton was followed up with the June 1995 Gore–Chernomyrdin framework. Ambiguity reigned, however, as to what the earlier contracts entailed. Often U.S. analysts surmised that Moscow was using the agreement as a basis to conduct new deals. Furthermore,

Russian commentators alluded openly to ways of circumventing the 1994 commitment to the United States,[38] and arms transfers continued after the 1999 deadline.

This framework completely collapsed in November 2000, when Foreign Minister Igor Ivanov informed Secretary of State Madeleine Albright that Russia was canceling its previous commitment to the United States and planning to renew arms contracts with Iran. This announcement was followed by the December 2000 visit to Iran by the Russian delegation of then-Defense Minister Sergeyev. The delegation accompanying the minister included Colonel General Leonid Ivashov, who heads the main directorate for international military cooperation at the Russian Defense Ministry, and senior representatives of the Russian State Company for the Export of Arms and Military Equipment (Rosoboroneksport).

Clearly, arms sales were a major item on the agenda of this visit. According to Viktor Komardin, head of Rosoboroneksport, the two states discussed "concrete questions" during Sergeyev's visit.[39] Ivashov announced during the visit that Putin himself was directing the new military contacts.[40] The IRNA reported that

> [At this meeting], according to Sergeyev, the two states assessed the state of security in Central Asia and in the North Caucasus, adjusted our positions on international security issues, evaluated them, compared conclusions as to the development of military cooperation, and have come to see that our positions are very close.[41]

With the termination of Russia's commitment to the United States not to conclude new arms agreements with Tehran, and with Iran's increased ability to pay for weapons, thanks to high oil prices, there may be a significant increase in the extent of arms sales between the two countries in 2001. Iran's ambassador to Russia, Mehdi Safari, stated in a February 2001 interview with the Russian newspaper *Rossiiskaia Gazeta* that Iran intends to purchase approximately $7 billion worth of arms from Russia in the coming years.[42] Iranian defense minister 'Ali Shamkhani also confirmed that Iran and Russia intend to expand their cooperation in security, military, and defense matters; he termed it "a must."[43] The two agreed during the Sergeyev visit that Iranian personnel would be trained at Russian military schools, studying Russian tactics and equipment. This could contribute to the institutionalization of military cooperation between the two countries.[44]

Russian Reactions to U.S. Nonproliferation Efforts

The Clinton administration made aggressive attempts to curtail Russian cooperation with Tehran in fields that could advance Iran's WMD program. Washington adopted a strategy of dealing with Iran's potential suppliers. The United States has successfully curbed the cooperation of a number of states, such as Ukraine and China, but it has been less successful with Russia. Commentators have pointed to the general decline in Russian–U.S. relations and more specifically to the U.S. decision to expand NATO eastward as triggers in Russia's decision to supply arms to Iran. But in fact Russia has supported the sale of arms and technology to Iran since at least the beginning of the post-Soviet era. Even during the height of the Russian–U.S. honeymoon, Russia attempted to complete its 1989 deal with Tehran and sell additional arms to Iran.

U.S. policymakers assumed in the early 1990s that Russia would keenly cooperate with their own efforts to thwart Iran's acquisition of weapons systems and progress in WMD programs. Such cooperation was presumably in line with Moscow's own security interests as a state adjacent to Iran, especially at a time when Washington perceived imminent clashes between Russia and Iran over Central Asia and the Caucasus. But from the very beginning, Moscow's perception of its security interests differed greatly from the U.S. perception of them.

In order to serve as a constructive partner in the nonproliferation efforts, Moscow has to view those efforts as advancing its own interests, not as a concession to the United States. In fact, Russia began to see its arms sales and technology cooperation with Iran as symbolic of its defiance against the United States and emblematic of its independent foreign policy. Chairman of the Duma Committee on International Affairs Vladimir Lukin stated, "Concern expressed by official Washington in connection with the Russian–Iranian agreement on the delivery of nuclear reactors to Iran cannot and must not be a subject of Russian–American talks."[45]

In response to the U.S. declaration of sanctions on Russian companies that had exported to Iran materials and technology that advance WMD programs, the Duma announced its rejection of "interference by third countries" in Russian–Iranian relations and its approval of a statement "On Expanding Cooperation between the Russian Federation and the Islamic Republic of Iran."[46] Moreover, in Moscow the discussion has evolved from one on commitment to the world nonproliferation regime and its implications on Russian security and interests to one on the appropriate response to U.S. pressure. For instance, in response to the fall 1999 U.S. congressional decision to apply sanctions on additional Russian companies accused of cooperating with Iranian companies in fields that could advance their WMD programs, the Russian Foreign Ministry declared that the decision would "have the most negative impact on the U.S.–Russian cooperation in the fields of nonproliferation and exports control."[47]

Throughout the 1990s, Russia was rarely straightforward about its intentions to supply Iran with either conventional- or nuclear-relevant technologies and equipment. Generally speaking, only when the United States revealed its discovery of deals between Iran and Russia did Moscow concede their existence. This trend was evident in the supply of the Kilo submarines to Iran, which Russian officials had repeatedly denied.[48] Iranian officials also attempted to hide aspects of their security cooperation with Russia. For instance, in the face of hard evidence of a Russian agreement to supply Iran with a gas centrifuge, former head of the Atomic Energy Organization of Iran, Dr. Reza Amrollahi said:

The centrifuge is a machine for enriching fuel. It was never a part of our agreement . . . There is international propaganda. As you know, the Russians also said that the centrifuge is not a part of our work.[49]

Yet even as Moscow extols the integrity of Iran's commitments to nonproliferation, its security organizations target Iranians in Russia, and Federal Security Service (FSB) spokesmen announce that they have discovered and foiled Iranian attempts to acquire Russian materials and technologies illicitly.[50] These detections illustrate that Iran is attempting to acquire what it cannot procure within the more transparent process of trade. FSB representative Major General Alexander Zdanovich stated that in May 1998, the FSB presented the Russian government ministries with a list of foreign companies operating in Russia that are "involved in military programs in the sphere of manufacturing WMD and delivery systems."[51] The FSB had thwarted attempts at violating the export controls "by certain state and private Iranian companies which tried to gain access to dual-purpose commodities and services by circumventing existing regulations."[52] In a 1998 interview with *Rossiiskaia Gazeta*, Zdanovich discussed the involvement of visiting Iranian students from Sanam college in espionage activities inside Russia:

[Sanam College] representatives [from Iran] have repeatedly tried to obtain information about Russian developments in the sphere of space, missile, nuclear, aviation, and laser technology. The Iranian side was informed of the unacceptability of such actions on Russian territory in January. As a result, Sanam's activity in our country has now stopped. The studies in the Baltic State Technical University of a group of Iranian students sent to St. Petersburg via the Sanam College organization have also been suspended. The possibility of continuing exchanges between higher educational institutions is being examined by the appropriate commission. Last year was a productive year for the detection of people trying to breach legislation on the export of dual-purpose goods and services. . . . In the capital, 'Aziz Mas'ud, a member of the Iranian military delegation, tried to obtain technical material on aviation matters from a Russian citizen. The foreigner was expelled from Russia in accordance with established practice.[53]

Iranian attempts to procure technologies illicitly, as well as Russia's violations of its own export laws, were particularly noticeable in the field of missile production.[54] As FSB chief, Vladimir Putin was clearly aware of the organization's policy to target Iran— and of its discoveries. Nevertheless, in a June 1999 meeting with the Iranian minister of interior, Putin stated that regarding cooperation on technology, "Moscow, despite all the external pressures which are aimed at limiting such cooperation, is committed to abide by agreements it has entered with the Islamic Republic of Iran."[55]

Notes

1. Robert J. Einhorn, assistant secretary of state for nonproliferation, testimony before the Senate Foreign Relations Committee, Washington, D.C., October 5, 2000 (hereafter Einhorn testimony); John A. Lauder, director, Directorate of Central Intelligence's Nonproliferation Center, statement before the Senate Committee on Foreign Relations on Russian proliferation to Iran's weapons of mass destruction and missile programs, October 5, 2000 (hereafter Lauder statement).

2. Vishniakov, "Russian–Iranian Relations and Regional Stability," p. 152.

3. See Anthony Cordesman, *Military Trends in Iran* (Washington, D.C.: Center for Strategic and International Studies, 1998); Michael Eisenstadt, *Iranian Military Power: Capabilities and Intentions*, Policy Papers no. 42 (Washington, D.C.: The Washington Institute for Near East Policy, 1996); "Unclassified Report to Congress on the Acquisition of Technology Relating to Weapons of Mass Destruction and Advanced Conventional Munitions, July 1 through December 31 1999," found at http://www.cia.gov/cia/publications/bian/bian_aug2000.htm#3; *Tracking Nuclear Proliferation 1998*, found at www.ceip.org.

4. Einhorn testimony.

5. Ibid.

6. Ibid.

7. *Priroda*, August 1995, no. 8, pp. 3-11 (interview with Viktor Mikhailov)

(FBIS-SOV-95-245-S); *Tehran Times,* May 9, 1995, p. 1 (interview with Kamal Kharrazi) (FBIS-NES-95-092).

8. Bushehr is located in southern Iran. In 1975, the German Siemens/Kraftwork Union (KWU) began construction of a nuclear power plant in Bushehr. This construction was halted with the advent of the Islamic Revolution in Iran. The site was seriously damaged in the Iran–Iraq War.

9. *Priroda,* August 1995, no. 8, pp. 3–11 (FBIS-SOV-95-245-S).

10. *Russian–Iranian Nuclear Cooperation Accord,* January 8, 1995, Natural Resources Defense Council (NRDC), reprinted in Eisenstadt, *Iranian Military Power,* pp. 108–109.

11. Weekly Compilation of Presidential Documents from the 1996 Presidential Documents, located at www.frwais.access.gpo.gov.

12. Itar-Tass, February 21, 2001.

13. Priroda, August 1995, no. 8, pp. 3–11 (FBIS-SOV-95-245-S).

14. Ibid.

15. Ibid.

16. IRNA in English, November 17, 1999; Itar-Tass in English, November 15, 1999.

17. Priroda, August 1995, no. 8, pp. 3–11 (FBIS-SOV-95-245-S). Russia eventually did begin to offer credit financing for its nuclear reactors, including reactors it sold to Iran.

18. See Eugene Rumer, *Dangerous Drift* (Washington, D.C.: Washington Institute for Near East Policy, 2000) for an extensive examination of the role that MINATOM and other Russian organizations and ministries play in Moscow's cooperation with Iran.

19. Adamov press briefing, August 26, 1999, Official Kremlin International News Broadcast, Adamov's speech at the Uranium Institute, September 1999, located at http://www.uilondon.org/sym/1999/adamov.htm; Itar-Tass, May 16, 2000; Adamov Press briefing September 12, 2000, Official Kremlin International News Broadcast.

20. For instance, in January 2000, Hasan Ruhani, Secretary of Iran's Supreme Council for National Security, headed a delegation to Moscow, which concluded a series of arms agreements, including an agreement on a supply of Mi-17 helicopters to Iran.

21. Vladimir Lukin, Russian Public Television First Channel, May 11, 1995 (FBIS-SOV-95-091).

22. *Abrar,* September 27, 1995 (FBIS-NES-95-196).

23. *Priroda,* August 1995, no. 8, pp. 3–11 (FBIS-SOV-95-245-S).

24. For instance, *Krasnaia Zvezda,* January 12, 1995; Interfax in English, February 15, 1995; Itar-Tass in English, February 22, 1995; *Kommersant-Daily,* March 11, 1995, p. 4 (FBIS-SOV-049).

25. Itar-Tass, June 16, 1998.

26. *Kommersant-Daily,* March 11, 1995, p. 4 (FBIS-SOV-049).

27. Testimony of Robert D. Walpole, National Intelligence for Strategic and Nuclear Programs, National Intelligence Council, before the U.S. Senate, Committee on Governmental Affairs, Subcommittee on International Security, Proliferation, and Federal Services, September 21, 2000. The Shahab-5 is a mock-up of a space launch vehicle, which is useable as an intercontinental ballistic missile. Iran has displayed the Shahab-5.

28. Lauder statement; Robert Galucci, "Iran–Russia Missile Cooperation: A United States View," in Joseph Cirincione, ed., *Repairing the Regime: Preventing the Spread of Weapons of Mass Destruction* (New York: Routledge, 2000), p. 188.

29. *New York Times,* February 8, 2001.

30. Einhorn testimony.

31. IRNA, December 27, 2000.

32. Itar-Tass, December 27, 2000.

33. Einhorn testimony; Lauder statement.

34. Lauder statement.

35. Ibid.

36. *Krasnaia Zvezda,* February 21, 1995, p. 3 (FBIS-SOV-95-039-S).

37. Anthony Cordesman, *Military Trends in Iran* (Washington, D.C.: Center for Strategic and International Studies, 1998), p. 13.

38. *Moskovskiye Novosti,* December 29, 1996; Interfax in English, February 3, 1997.

39. Reuters, February 11, 2001.

40. Itar-Tass, December 27, 2000.

41. IRNA, December 27, 2000.

42. Mehdi Safari, interview to *Rossiiskaia Gazeta,* quoted in RFE/RL *Newsline,* Vol. 5, No. 38, Part I, February 23, 2001.

43. IRNA, December 27, 2000.

44. Itar-Tass, December 28, 2000.

45. Itar-Tass, April 25, 1995 (FBIS-SOV-95-080). It should be noted that Lukin belongs to the Yabloko Party, which is one of the most staunchly pro-U.S. and liberal-oriented political parties in the Russian Duma.

46. Itar-Tass, October 21, 1998 (FBIS-SOV-98-294).

47. Itar-Tass in English, September 16, 1999.

48. TASS in English, March 24, 1992 (FBIS-SOV-92-059).

49. IRIB Television, May 14, 1995 (FBIS-NES-95-093).

50. Itar-Tass in English, January 14, 1999.

51. *Rossiiskaia Gazeta*, July 1, 1998, p. 8 (FBIS-SOV-98-182).

52. Interfax in English, May 28, 1998.

53. *Rossiiskaia Gazeta*, July 1, 1998, p. 8 (FBIS-SOV-98-182).

54. Itar-Tass, April 10, 1998; *Obshchaia Gazeta*, May 7–13, 1998, p. 6 (FBIS-SOV-98-139); The White House, Office of the Press Secretary, Fact Sheet, September 2, 1998.

55. IRNA in English, June 30, 1999.

Chapter 5
Policy Implications and Conclusions

Russia and Iran view their mutual relations as an important component of the national security and regime stability of their respective states. The close cooperation between Tehran and Moscow has been made possible by both states' pragmatic and nonideological approaches toward each other. Iran's interactions with Russia regarding the Chechnya and Nagorno–Karabagh conflicts demonstrate that its geostrategic interests concerning Russia clearly override its declared commitment to Islamic solidarity. Its assessments of those interests inform its cooperation with Russia, and the two sides have rarely clashed over issues connected with the Muslim populations of Russia, Central Asia, or the Caucasus. Many U.S. observers have assumed that Russia and Iran would collide in the latter two regions. In order to form an appropriate policy toward these two states and their mutual cooperation, the United States must recognize the pragmatic concerns behind this relationship. Cultural and religious affinities have had little impact on Iran and Russia's mutual and regional relations.

Russia does not view Iran as a serious threat to its security interests. In areas where it perceives that the two countries could clash, Moscow sees cooperation with Tehran as a means of preempting potential Iranian threats. Chechnya is a case in point. To ensure that Iran would check Muslim hostility toward Russia over its actions in Chechnya, Moscow often tried to provide Tehran with certain rewards. Its commitments to supply Iran with conventional military supplies and nuclear reactors surged during heightened periods of confrontation in Chechnya.

In light of the importance Moscow and Tehran attach to their mutual relations, Moscow cannot be relied upon to serve as an ally in Washington's nonproliferation efforts with regard to Iran. This study has shown that Russia is fully aware of Iran's attempts to acquire weapons of mass destruction (WMD) and has responded to them with a relaxed attitude. Because of the high priority Russia attaches to its relations with Iran—an important "pole" in its attempt to create a multipolar world system—it has been unwilling to curtail its cooperation for minimal financial incentives from the United States. Thus the threat and implementation of limited U.S. sanctions against Russia have not served as an effective deterrent. Moreover, U.S. threats have often involved the cancellation of programs that are important to the United States but not to Russia—such as financial aid for the storage and destruction of fissile materials. In fact, the policy of linking nonproliferation concerns to these assistance programs pose a triple threat for the United States: it fails to stop the cooperation between Russia and Iran, it undermines an important program to advance nonproliferation and safety efforts, and it compromises U.S. credibility.

Russia will not halt its cooperation with Iran unless it sees it as in its own interest instead of as a concession to the United States. In contrast, financial incentives and the imposition of sanctions have been effective in modifying the behavior of individual Russian companies and institutions and have contributed to nonproliferation efforts. This policy may continue to be an effective way to deal with activities not sanctioned by the central Russian government.

In addition, Washington could consider focusing more narrowly on those elements of Russian–Iranian cooperation that are most disturbing. For instance, conventional arms sales to Iran are less of a threat to the interests of the United States and its allies than are WMD or missiles. Iran needs a strong army so that it can deal with regional threats and feel more secure—and thus possibly less motivated to acquire WMD. Plus, Moscow needs this potential source of income. Washington's demands regarding conventional arms must be perceived by Russia as reasonable.

Another possible strategy is for the United States to approach President Vladimir Putin about limited and quiet cooperation on these types of issues. Before his ascent to the presidency, Putin personally oversaw much of Russia's cooperation with Iran. He has strong knowledge of Russia's dealings with Iran and regards the relationship as an important one. Regarding U.S. efforts to limit Russia's cooperation with Iran, Putin will bargain a lot harder than did his predecessor. Boris Yeltsin tended to agree to U.S. demands but did little to uphold them. Putin knows the issues well and knows what enforcement measures the agreements entail. He is likely to agree to less, and to exact a higher price for cooperation (potentially in larger areas of disarmament issues, which could further complicate the issue), but he will be more serious in enforcing the agreements he commits to.

Signs have emerged to the effect that Putin, under whose rule many Russian policies have become centralized and more firmly articulated, is establishing a coherent policy toward cooperation with Iran, and that there will be fewer of the policy meanderings characteristic of previous eras. For instance, Putin has renewed efforts to enforce and reinforce Russia's export control laws. In February 2001 he told the Russian Security Council that improving the country's export control system was "the most important [way] of ensuring the country's security" and emphasized the necessity of preventing the outflow of dual-use items from Russia.[1]

Taking into account the wide spectrum of opposition in Russia (even among pro-U.S. political forces) to Washington's dictates regarding its foreign affairs, Putin's cooperation on nonproliferation is best elicited through nonpublic channels. The Russian president is building his political base on Russian patriotism and reasserted foreign policy independence. He will not give the appearance of deferring to U.S. pressure on an issue involving Russian national interests. Moreover, Putin is committed to pursuing cooperative relations with Iran. But in light of his FSB background and that organization's knowledge of Iran's illicit efforts to acquire technologies and equipment, Putin may be willing to cooperate on limited and focused nonproliferation efforts, provided they are carried out quietly and not perceived as responses to U.S. pressure.

Relying on quiet diplomacy has its drawbacks, of course. First, Russia may infer that the United States has downgraded the issue of Iranian proliferation, and so may conclude that it need not do much to cooperate with Washington. Second, high-profile policy on this issue has focused more U.S. media and congressional attention toward Russian–Iranian cooperation, which has led to efforts to uncover clandestine cooperation between the two countries.

Since the Soviet Union's demise, Russia's "lines in the sand" have shifted a number of times. Positions it was not willing to accept in the early 1990s have become palatable with time, as Russia has adjusted to a new strategic posture and challenges. Accordingly, the United States would be wise to constantly update its policies toward Russia and not to assume that Russian policy patterns characteristic of the 1990s will necessarily continue.

This study has emphasized that Russia and Iran share a strategic partnership and perceive their relationship as important to their own national security. These strategic relations, however, are based on the assumption that Russia and Iran operate in a unipolar world, where each country has problematic relations with the United States. If these conditions were to change and one or both of them were to develop excellent relations with the United States, the relationship between Russia and Iran could change dramatically as well. Russia would stand to lose from a rapprochement between Tehran and the United States. Yet these relations do not have to be viewed as zero-sum. The United States and Russia are not necessarily competitive in every zone and sphere they cohabit. If the United States improves its relations with Iran, it should consider including Russia in this process and updating Moscow on the steps Washington takes with Tehran. In addition, there are some areas, such as Afghanistan, where the interests of Tehran, Moscow, and

Washington are complementary. The United States has much to gain from trilateral cooperation where it is possible.

Note

1. Itar-Tass, quoted in RFE/RL Newsline 5, no. 38, part I, February 23, 2001.